Learning to Read Music

More related titles

Touch Typing in Ten Hours
Spend a few hours now and gain a valuable skill for life

'It works! Even if you are a two-fingered, search-and-hunt, typist you can learn to touch type if you follow the ten one-hour exercises.' – *Writers' News*

Our Greatest Writers
and their major works

This book will take you to the heart of some of the great literature of the English language. Our major writers are presented in order of their birth, and discussed through carefully selected extracts, informed comment and key bibliographic detail; giving you the opportunity to discover some of the finest writers of the English language and be able to speak about them and their writing with confidence.

'A perfect tool for upping your literary IQ.' – *The Good Book Guide*

'Excellent...a useful, well-written book.' – *The Teacher*

Holiday Courses for Long Weekends and Short Breaks
A guide to the best holiday courses and workshops in the UK and Ireland

A unique guide full of fascinating and often unusual things you can do on your next holiday. Gain a new skill, pursue an exciting hobby, or develop an interest you already have.

howtobooks

Please send for a free copy of the latest catalogue:

How To Books
3 Newtec Place, Magdalen Road, Oxford OX4 1RE, United Kingdom
email: info@howtobooks.co.uk
http://www.howtobooks.co.uk

Learning to Read Music

Make sense of those mysterious symbols and bring music alive

Peter Nickol

howto**books**

Published by How To Books Ltd
3 Newtec Place, Magdalen Road
Oxford OX4 1RE, United Kingdom
Tel: (01865) 793806 Fax: (01865) 248780
email: info@howtobooks.co.uk
www.howtobooks.co.uk

First edition 1999
Reprinted 2002
Second edition 2005

British Library Cataloguing in Publication Data.
A catalogue record for this book is available from the British Library.

Cover design by Baseline Arts Ltd, Oxford
Produced for How To Books by Deer Park Productions, Tavistock
Type and music set by Peter Nickol
Printed and bound by Bell & Bain Ltd, Glasgow

NOTE: The material contained in this book is set out in good faith for general
guidance and no liability can be accepted for loss or expense incurred as a result
of relying in particular circumstances on statements made in the book. Laws and
regulations are complex and liable to change, and readers should check the
current position with the relevant authorities before making personal
arrangements.

Contents

Spot the Dot

Our systematic look at how to read music starts on page 11. On these two pages, for easy reference, is a 'spot the dot' visual index of music symbols. Beside each symbol is its name, and the page number where its purpose and use are first explained.

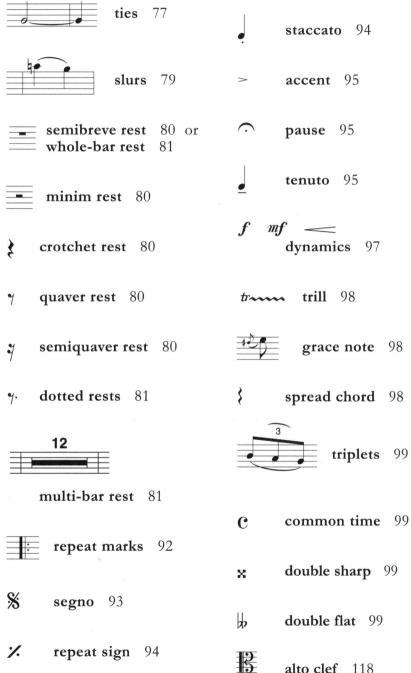

Preface

This is a handbook for anyone who would like to read music.

You don't have to play an instrument. It helps, because practising your instrument reinforces your music-reading and makes it less abstract. But it's not essential. You may have other reasons for wanting to read music – for instance, if you sing in a choir, or would like to follow scores while listening, or if your work brings you into contact with printed music.

As you read this book you will find some stages easier than others. The difficult bits, for most people, are rhythms and keys. They are difficult because we are trying to put down on paper something which is uniquely musical, and unlike almost anything else.

But there are good reasons why music gets written down. Not all music needs it, but most classical music would be impossible to play without being notated. Most pop and jazz musicians, also, are quick to commend the value of learning to read music.

So… work your way through the difficult bits, and with a bit of persistence you'll get there in the end. Good luck!

Peter Nickol

1

High or Low

On a page of printed music, most of the symbols, and the way they are positioned, concern two things:

◆ **Pitch**
High or low notes; whether a note is C, D, E or whatever

◆ **Duration**
Whether notes are long or short; how they relate to each other in *time*

We'll start in this chapter with **pitch**.

WHAT IS PITCH?

In music we talk of sounds being 'high' or 'low' – meaning high-pitched or low-pitched. You probably know this instinctively, but high-pitched sounds are those made at the right-hand end of a piano keyboard, or by high-pitched instruments such as piccolo or descant recorder. Low-pitched sounds come from the left-hand end of the piano, or from instruments such as double-bass or tuba.

THE STAVE

When music is written down, the **stave** (or **staff**) – a set of five horizontal lines – is a way of indicating high or low:

 ↑ higher

↓ lower

Notes can be positioned on the lines:

or in the spaces:

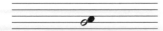

Ledger lines

The five-line stave can be extended upwards or downwards by using **ledger lines**:

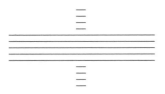

Notes can be put on or between the ledger lines:

Higher and lower notes

These two notes are very close together – but the black note is a little higher than the white note:

These two are further apart:

and these two are still further apart:

but in each case the black note is the higher one.

CLEFS

But what notes are they, those notes? What are they called? We don't know. We only know how far apart they are, *relative to each other*.

In order to give the notes a more fixed identity, we must attach a **clef** to the **stave**.

This is a **treble clef**:

And this is a **bass clef**: 𝄢

There are other clefs, but those two are by far the most commonly used.

USING A CLEF FIXES THE PITCH

When we put a clef on a stave, it has the effect of *fixing* or *identifying* the pitch of the lines and spaces. For instance, if we put a treble clef on a stave, like this:

we can then put a name to each note – each line and each space. The bottom line, for instance, is E:

And these are F and G:

F   G

More precisely still, we can call the bottom line 'the E above middle C', to distinguish it from other Es. Middle C itself is written on the first ledger line below the stave:

Putting a *bass* clef on the stave also fixes the pitches of the lines and spaces, but at a different, lower pitch range. The top line, for instance, is A – 'A below middle C':

And this is middle C, using the bass clef:

WHAT DO WE MEAN BY 'MIDDLE C'?

Finding C on a piano

Look at this diagram of a piano keyboard:

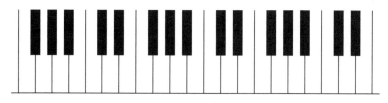

Keyboard players orientate themselves by looking at the pattern of black notes – alternate twos and threes. They need to do this even if they are only playing white notes.

C is *always* just to the left of the *two* black notes. Every white note to the left of a pair of black notes is a C:

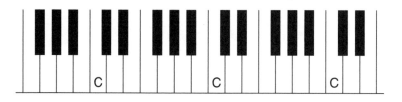

Middle C

The C nearest the middle of any piano is called 'middle C'.

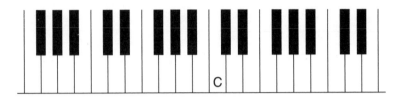

There's nothing special about middle C. It's just one note, *a particular pitch*.

But by giving that note a special name – a name that distinguishes it from other notes, even other Cs – we gain a point of reference. And that point of reference applies to all music, not just piano music.

Incidentally, middle C is always near the middle of a true piano keyboard, but electronic keyboards are sometimes laid out differently. Middle C may be quite far over to the left – or its position may be electronically switchable.

'Higher' or 'lower' – on a piano

When you sit facing a piano keyboard, the higher notes are on your right, the lower ones on your left. This may seem obvious to you, but it's worth being clear about. When we play 'upwards' on the piano we play notes from left to right. 'Downwards' is from right to left.

Going up from middle C

If we play five white notes on a piano, starting on middle C and going 'up' (rightwards), this is what we play:

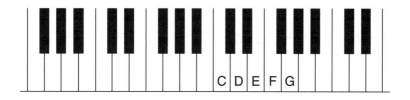

If we write five notes on a stave with a treble clef, also starting on middle C and going up, we write the same five notes:

NOTE-NAMES

To identify the notes, to give them 'names', we use the first seven letters of the alphabet, A to G. As we've seen, if we start at middle C and go up, step by step, we get D, E, F and G. But the next note up is A, and the cycle of seven letters starts again:

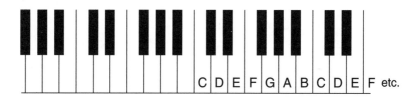

In notation, the same notes look like this:

Look again at the pattern of black and white notes on the keyboard. The five black notes mesh with seven white notes, corresponding to the seven letter names A to G. This is why C, or any other note, always recurs in the same position relative to the black notes.

Going down from middle C

Similarly, if we go *down* from middle C, this is what we get:

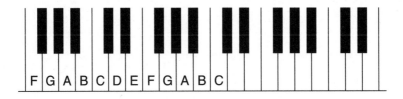

We could start writing this with the treble clef:

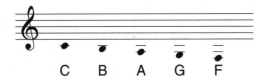

but we'd need more and more ledger lines. The bass clef is a lot more suitable, because of the pitch range:

We read music just like we read words: from left to right. When you look at the stave above, you are reading a descending series of notes, starting with middle C. Of course, when you look at the same notes on the keyboard diagram, further above, they appear from right to left, because the lowest notes are at the left end of a keyboard.

WHY THE SEVEN-NOTE PATTERN RECURS

When you play the notes on a piano (or any instrument) from A up to G, why is the next note A again and not H? Why *does* that sequence of seven notes keep repeating as one goes up or down in pitch?

It's an important thing to understand, and if possible you should *hear* the reason. So even if you don't play or own an instrument, please try to borrow or gain access to one for this particular exercise.

Listening to notes with the same name

Once you have access to an instrument, play several different Cs. For instance, if you have a piano, play middle C, then the C above, then the C below. (Use the keyboard diagrams to help you find C. Look at the pattern of the black notes. C is always just left of the *two* black notes.) Listen closely.

In one sense the Cs are different from each other, because one is clearly higher or lower than another. But in a different sense they are specially similar, and that's why they share the same note-name. Can you hear that similarity? Play other notes for comparison.

Then repeat the exercise using As instead of Cs.

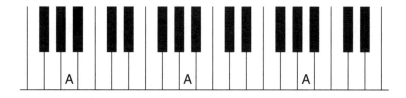

Again, you should find that although two different As differ in pitch – one is higher or lower than the other – they are in another sense similar, almost the same. It's one of the things about music that's difficult to describe in words.

The scientific explanation

There is actually a scientific reason why the two Cs (or two As, or whichever note you're listening to) sound similar despite being at different pitches. It's to do with *vibrations*, and *frequency* of vibration.

All sounds are vibrations. They reach the ear through vibrations of the air. A sound with a regular pitch (an identifiable *note*) has *regular* vibrations; unpitched noise has *irregular* vibrations.

High-pitched sounds vibrate faster than low-pitched sounds. And the crucial point here is that middle C vibrates *exactly half as fast* as the next C *up*; similarly, it vibrates exactly *twice* as fast as the next C *down*. That's why the Cs sound similar to each other: their frequencies have a particular and close mathematical relationship.

Three consecutive As on the piano have the same relationship to each other, even though the actual frequencies are different. The highest has twice the frequency of the middle one, which in turn has twice the frequency of the lowest.

OCTAVES

The distance from one C to the next C, up or down, is called **one octave**.

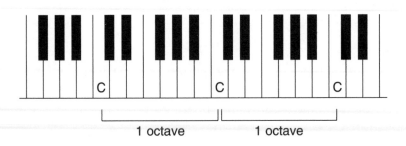

1 octave   1 octave

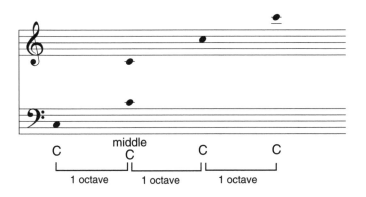

You will appreciate the meaning of *two octaves*:

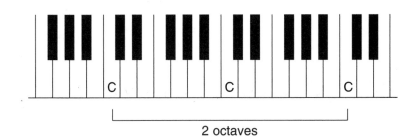

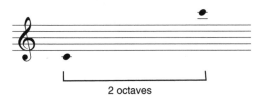

Octaves don't just go from C to C, they exist from *any* note to another note with the same letter-name:

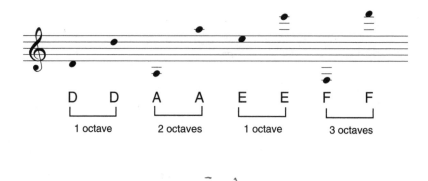

TEST YOURSELF

Look at all these notes. Try to remember all of them – which lines or spaces they use.

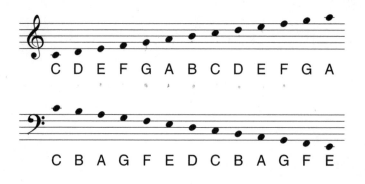

Now look at the octave examples at the top of the page. Are all the notes correctly labelled? (Yes, they are – but please check for yourself, especially those awkward notes with lots of ledger lines.)

It's time to test yourself. Cover up the opposite page; then look at the notes below and on the next page, and say what they are. You should become gradually quicker at identifying them as you work your way through this exercise. Remember: always look to see which clef you're in. (Even the best musicians sometimes play the wrong notes because they have forgotten which clef they're in.) Answers on page 126.

How did you do with the note-naming exercise? Always remember the importance of the clef: the lines and spaces have no intrinsic pitch until there's a clef there to fix the pitches.

One more test: look back through the note-naming exercise and pick out all the times that middle C is printed. Again, you can check your answer on page 126.

How absolute is pitch?

Defining pitch is a funny business. We've said that Middle C is a certain note on a piano, or indeed as played on any other instrument. But if we play Middle C on two different instruments we may get two slightly different notes, depending on the instruments and how they've been tuned. Is one of them right and one wrong? Is there an absolute pitch for Middle C, independent of any instrument?

Not really. Middle C, and other notes, do not have an absolute value: they can vary slightly from one instrument to another, from one country to another, and have certainly varied from one century to another. We can tell this by examining instruments, for instance church organs, from different times and places.

In practice, though, music (like everything else) is becoming ever more internationally standardised. One standard pitch-definition we have is that the A above Middle C is a note whose sound-waves vibrate at 440 cycles per second. If you buy a tuning fork, it will probably comply with that standard.

In the context of this book, none of this matters much. The imortant thing is that whenever musicians play together, they should be in tune with each other. Fine adjustments are often required, and this is what the 'tuning up' session at the start of an orchestral concert is about.

Pitch, in music, is almost always a matter of *relative* pitch, from one note to another, rather than absolute pitch, as measured in vibrations per second.

POINTS TO REMEMBER

1 This chapter deals with **pitch** – high or low.

2 Notes go on the **stave** – on or between the lines – or on **ledger lines** above or below the stave.

3 To 'fix' the notes, we put a **clef** on the stave. The most common clefs are **treble** and **bass**.

4 On a piano, C is just to the left of the two black notes.

5 On a piano, the lower notes are to the left, the higher notes to the right.

6 The white notes on a piano are named from A to G.

7 From one A to the next A (up or down) is **one octave**. Octaves go from one note to another note with the same note-name.

8 Always look to see what clef you're in.

2

Long or Short

DURATION

Now you know how music symbols are used to indicate **pitch** – how high or low a note is.

Next, we consider **duration** – how long or short it is.

The different shapes used for printing notes

So far, we've just used note-heads on the stave, to indicate which pitch is referred to. But on a page of printed music you will see a wide variety of note-symbols. Here are some of the common ones:

These symbols indicate durations, but they do so in *relative* terms, not *absolute* terms. In other words, the symbols indicate how long the notes last *relative to each other*, not how long they last in seconds or fractions of a second.

NOTE-VALUES

Semibreve, minim, crotchet, quaver

We can set out a simple chart of relative note-values, as shown below. Study the chart, and try to memorise the terms for the different note-shapes, as described below the chart and on the next page. 'Whole note', 'half note' (etc) is the terminology used in America, and neatly expresses the relationships between the notes, but 'semibreve', 'minim' (etc) is also a terminology you need to know, and is the usual one in Britain.

At the top you can see one *whole note* or **semibreve**.

Then two *half notes* or **minims**.

The third line has four *quarter notes* or **crotchets**.

The fourth line has eight *eighth notes* or **quavers**.

And the fifth line shows sixteen *sixteenth notes* or **semiquavers**.

The chart shows their relative values. The two minims 'add up' to the one semibreve. Similarly the four crotchets 'add up' to the two minims or one semibreve. And so on. All five lines have the same total time-value.

UNDERSTANDING RELATIVE TIME-VALUES

Do you understand how the matter of relative time-values works? Music may be fast or slow. A particular piece of music may be taken at a faster or slower tempo. A crotchet, or a minim, or a quaver, may be fast or slow. But, *at any one time, whatever the tempo*, a crotchet is *always* half as long (or twice as fast) as a minim, and a quaver is *always* half as long (or twice as fast) as a crotchet.

INDICATING FAST OR SLOW

Is it impossible, then, for the *absolute* duration of notes to be indicated? Surely composers will sometimes want to do that, to indicate how fast or slow they want their music.

Yes, it is possible, and composers use various ways of getting this information across.

Metronome marks

One normal – and quite precise – method is to place a **metronome mark** at the head of the score. (A metronome is a clock-like mechanism that ticks at any required speed.) Having written out their composition, with all the relative note-values notated, the composer then writes at the top something like this:

$$\text{♩} = 96$$

This means that the music should be played at 96 crotchets per minute. That is the *absolute* speed (or **tempo**). All the *relative* note-values – the crotchets, quavers, minims, etc. – then take place at that speed.

Setting an exact absolute tempo carries certain problems. The composer may want the tempo to fluctuate in subtle ways, or the circumstances of a performance (e.g. the size and resonance of the room) may suggest a faster or slower tempo. In any case performers don't expect to be straightjacketed, and tempo is an area in which they normally have some interpretive leeway.

Accordingly a composer may add c. (for *circa*, = approximately) into a metronome mark:

$$\text{♩} = \text{c. } 96$$

Tempo marks

More commonly, there may be no metronome mark at the head of a score, but a tempo instruction in words – conventionally (though not necessarily) in Italian. For instance:

Allegro (fast)
Adagio (slow)
Andante (at walking pace)

Instructions of this sort may seem vague compared with '96 crotchets per minute', but in practice they can give a good idea of the composer's intentions.

More precise instructions have also evolved, for instance:

Allegro ma non troppo (fast, but not too fast)

Some terms carry a message about expression as well as tempo, e.g.

Largamente (broadly)

BEAMED NOTES

Two adjacent quavers can be beamed together, like this:

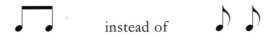

Or three quavers, or four, or even more.

Similarly, semiquavers can be beamed together:

A quaver followed by two semiquavers may be notated like this:

DOTTED NOTES

A dot written after a notehead multiplies the time-value by 1½.

So, a **dotted crotchet** ♩· = 3 quavers

A **dotted minim** ♩· = 3 crotchets

A **dotted quaver** ♪· = 3 semiquavers

A dotted quaver followed by a semiquaver can be beamed together, like this:

TEST YOURSELF

Time to check your knowledge of note-values. Here is one semibreve:

All but one of the following groups of notes have the same total duration as one semibreve. Check each line, adding up the time-values, and find out which line *does not* add up to one semibreve. (Answer on page 126.)

POINTS TO REMEMBER

1 This chapter is about **duration** – long or short.

2 The different shapes used for writing notes are called by names such as **crotchet, minim, quaver, semibreve**. These indicate durations, but they indicate *relative* durations.

3 Two semiquavers add up to one quaver, two quavers to one crotchet, two crotchets to one minim and two minims to one semibreve.

4 Speed is indicated by **metronome marks**, which indicate the speed more or less exactly, or by **tempo marks**, which indicate the *feel* required.

5 Adjacent quavers or semiquavers, in various combinations, are often beamed together.

6 Dotted notes are worth one-and-a-half times as much (in time-value) as the same note without the dot.

Music – existing in its own time and space

In Chapter 1 we saw that pitch is a relative matter. Within limits, the absolute pitch-standard of a performance doesn't matter much, but it is most important that all the players are in tune *with each other*. Likewise, an unaccompanied singer may start a song on C, D, E or whatever, but the melody thereafter proceeds along a set path.

Now, in Chapter 2, we discover that timing in music is also relative. Performances of the standard classical repertoire vary considerably in tempo, and hence in overall duration. Even given a metronome mark, the tempo of a performance may in practice turn out slightly faster or slightly slower. Yet the *internal* time-relationships, of the different notes to each other, matters to the tiniest fraction of a second.

Music can connect in the most intimate way with our lives and our feelings, but a musical performance is a remarkably self-contained thing, defined by internal relationships of time and pitch.

3

Rhythm and Beat

BEATS AND ACCENTS

The **note-values** you have learnt about in Chapter 2 work hand in hand with **time signatures**. With these two elements, composers notate everything to do with *rhythm* and *beat*.

A time signature sets up a *regular pattern of accents*. Let's examine how this works.

A regular beat

First, imagine a slowly ticking clock:

t   t   t   t   t   t   t   t   t

Say the 't's quietly to yourself, keeping them absolutely regular.

Adding accents

Now do it again, but this time give a little extra emphasis to every fourth 't', like this:

t   t   t   t   **t**   t   t   t   **t**

Your 't's should still be completely regular in time, but with every fourth one *accented*. The time signature of a piece of music describes its underlying metre, or pattern of beats and accents. Each 't' is a beat, and in this case every fourth 't' is an accented beat.

BEAT AND TEMPO (SPEED)

Before we look at time signatures in detail, we need to be clear about **tempo**, or speed.

The pattern of 't's (with every fourth 't' accented) might be fast or it might be slow. Say the 't's to yourself, following these tempo instructions:

fast

t   t   t   t   **t**   t   t   t   **t**

slow

t   t   t   t   **t**   t   t   t   **t**

Supposing the 't's were written closer together (or further apart)

It would be possible to write the 't's closer together for the fast version, like this:

fast

t t t t **t** t t t **t**

It seems reasonable, because it *looks* faster. But conventional music notation doesn't work like that. You have to look at the **time-values of the notes** (which you have been learning), the **time signature** (which we are coming to) and the **tempo indication** (e.g. 'allegro' or 'fast'). How close together the notes are printed is not important.

PRACTISING DIFFERENT METRES (BEAT-PATTERNS)

Now try putting the accent on every *third* 't'. Choose a comfortable speed, not too fast, and make sure your 't's are absolutely regular in time.

t t t **t** t t **t** t t **t** t t **t**

And now, put the accent on every *second* 't'.

t t **t** t **t** t **t** t **t**

You could even try accenting every *fifth* 't', even though in music this pattern is much less common.

t t t t t **t** t t t t **t** t t t t **t**

INTERNALISING THE BEAT

It's useful to be able to *internalise* (hear inside your head) the steady ticking beat of the music. Here are some patterns to practise. After you have said them out loud, try to hear them in your head, without actually making a sound. This will be much easier if all is quiet around you, without music or distracting noise in the background. Go through these patterns several times.

quite fast
t t t **t** t t **t** t t **t**

slow
t t t t **t** t t t **t** t t t **t**

(There are two more on the next page.)

very slow

t t t t t t t t t t t t t

very fast

t t t t t t t t t t t t t

You will appreciate that these tempo indications are not precise. If it says 'fast', *exactly* how fast is up to you. But once you have decided on a speed, keep it steady, keep the ticks regular.

As mentioned before, it is possible to set the tempo more precisely, for instance like this:

slow (60 't's per minute)

t t t t t t t t t t t t t

quite fast (120 't's per minute)

t t t t t t t t t t t t t

Try saying these accent-patterns, keeping to the stated tempo. If you have a watch or clock that marks the seconds, visually or audibly, use that to keep in time.

Again, start by saying the 't's out loud. Then internalise them, so that you can distinctly imagine, or hear in your head, the regular beat and the accents.

Go back to the four examples above, starting at the bottom of page 27, and go through them again. For each one, when you have settled on your tempo, check against a clock to see exactly how fast/slow it is, in beats per minute. (Often, that's how a composer decides what metronome mark to put at the head of a score.)

THE NATURE OF BEAT

All those examples will help you to understand time signatures. They are concerned with defining the metre or beat-pattern.

As you have realised, the **beat** (or **pulse**) of a piece of music can be fast or slow. Even if the tempo changes – for instance if the piece gradually speeds up, or there's a sudden change of tempo – basically the musician thinks of the beat as something steady, like a ticking clock, against which other things in the music happen.

GROUPING BEATS IN BARS

Each 't' is a beat. And each accented 't' marks the first beat in a **bar** (or **measure**, which is the American terminology).

Bars and barlines

Bars are separated by vertical lines called barlines:

Here are some barlines on an empty stave, just to show what they look like:

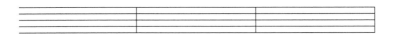

But for the moment we are concerned only with duration, not pitch, so we don't need the stave.

Now let's replace those 't's with proper notes.

Using notes as beats

Look at the next four examples. *All of them have three beats in each bar.*

Slow

Very slow

Fast

Fast

Looking at these four examples yields two important points:

◆ A beat might be a minim, or a crotchet, or a quaver. It might be any of them, or it might even be a semiquaver, or another note-value such as a dotted crotchet. Any note-value might be used to represent the beat.

◆ Don't assume that minims are always slower than crotchets, or crotchets slower than quavers. It's that business of relative time-values again: in a particular piece, at a particular moment, the quavers take exactly half as long as the crotchets, but when you are comparing two different pieces that relationship disappears.

The 't's – used to represent the regular ticking beat on the previous pages of this chapter – have now been replaced by notes. But those notes tick by in the same regular way, at a speed roughly indicated by the tempo mark at the beginning of each example.

Putting in barlines shows where the accents fall, by showing which is the first beat of each bar.

TIME SIGNATURES

Any note-value can be used to represent the beat – minim, crotchet, quaver, semquaver, dotted crotchet, dotted quaver, etc. A crotchet beat is the most common of all. But of course, it is very important that we know *which* note-value has been chosen.

That's where **time signatures** come in.

A time signature consists of two numbers, one above the other.

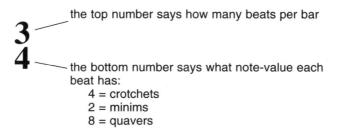

Understanding what time signatures mean, and how they work, is critical to reading music notation. We'll look at some examples of time signatures on the next page.

Examples of time signatures

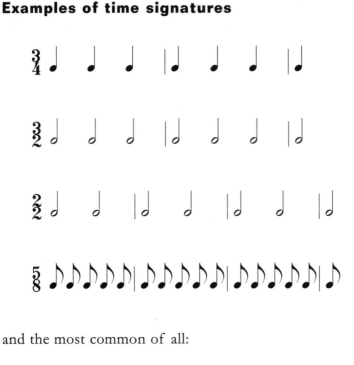

and the most common of all:

INTRODUCING RHYTHMS

The difference between rhythm and beat

Broadly speaking, we are using *beat* to mean something absolutely regular, like the ticking of a clock. (Some musicians prefer the word *pulse* to *beat*.) In the examples above, all the notes you can see are also beats. The first example has three crotchet beats in each bar, the second example has three minim beats in each bar, the third example has two minim beats in each bar, and so on.

Rhythm, on the other hand, is a word we use for something more complicated – not just a regular ticking beat, but a definite pattern, with some longer and some shorter notes. In other words, rhythms have a mixture of different note values.

Don't expect everyone to use those two words in quite that strict way. It's not a distinction that matters much in everyday language, so ordinary usage is a bit vaguer. Also, a pop musician might talk about different 'beats' where a classical musician would say 'rhythms'. But generally, dealing with music on a practical level, if someone refers to 'this rhythm' or 'that rhythm', then they mean *this* particular rhythmic pattern or *that* one. Or they might refer to the *pulse*, and then they mean the regular beat.

How different note-values fit against a beat

The next step is to start reading a variety of note-values against the background of a regular beat. Shorter notes may subdivide the beat, or longer ones may go across several beats.

The first few examples (on the next page) are all in $\frac{4}{4}$. That means there are four beats in each bar, and each beat is a crotchet.

Incidentally, to *say* a time signature, simply say the top number first: 'four four', 'three four' etc.

Also, when time signatures are printed in the middle of a passage of ordinary text, not on the stave, it's troublesome typographically to print the two numbers one above the other, as we have done a little further up this page. So normally, in ordinary text, they are printed with an oblique stroke like a fraction: 4/4. Always remember, though, that a time signature is not really a fraction at all, even if it looks a bit like one.

Back to the business in hand, which is reading different note-values against a regular beat. Start by establishing the steady beat in your head, or by tapping your foot. Choose a moderate tempo, and *feel* the regularity of the beat, as in a march. Give a slight emphasis to the first beat of each bar. Count the beats, like this:

1   2   3   4 |**1**   2   3   4 |**1**   2   3   4 |

Now read the four rhythms below, either in your head or by tapping or saying them in some way. The numbers above the notes show how the notes stand in relation to the beat.

The double barline at the end is just an indication of finality.

Rhythms in different time signatures

Now try reading some rhythms in other time signatures. Follow this procedure:

1   Look at the *top* number to see how many beats there are in each bar, and at the *bottom* number to see what time-value each beat has.
2   Then count the regular pattern of beats in your head, using the top number to tell you how many beats to count.
3   Finally read the rhythm against the background of the beats.

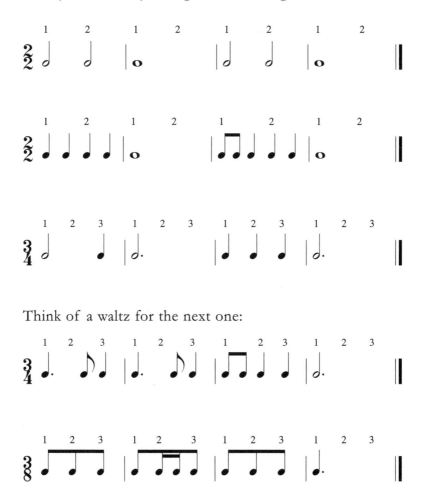

Think of a waltz for the next one:

Can read those rhythms? Can you tap them on a table, or hear them in your head? Go over them again if necessary, and don't be surprised if you find them difficult. It's not easy, trying to read or play a rhythm while keeping the regular beat mentally in the background.

POINTS TO REMEMBER

1 Musical **beat** or **pulse** is like the regular ticking of a clock.

2 Adding regular **accents** to the beat – for instance if every fourth beat is accented – creates a framework within which the rhythmic aspect of music can take place.

3 Beats are grouped in **bars**, the first beat of each bar being the accented one.

4 **Barlines** are vertical lines drawn through the stave to separate the bars.

5 The regular beat can be any speed, from very fast to very slow.

6 Any note-value can be used to represent a beat.

7 A **time signature** tells us two things. The top number tells us how many beats are in each bar. The bottom number tells us what note-value has been chosen to represent the beat: 4 = crotchets, 2 = minims, 8 = quavers. (There is an exception to this rule, which we will learn about later.)

8 Using time signatures and note-values, all sorts of rhythms can then be written down. The rhythms take place against the background of the regular beat.

4

Tunes

COMBINING PITCH AND RHYTHM

Now that you can read pitch *and* rhythm, you will realise how they work together. Here is a rhythm to be played or sung on the D just above middle C:

Here is the same rhythm an octave higher:

Stems: up or down?

It makes no difference whether the stems go up or down. Normally they go down if the note lies in the top half of the stave.

From rhythm to tune

Now here's the same rhythm using two notes, G and A:

And here it is again, using several notes:

By using several notes it becomes more melodic, more of a tune. If you can, play it on a piano or other instrument.

Here's another tune, this time in the bass clef:

Upbeats

One thing you may notice about this tune is that it begins on the fourth beat of the bar. It has been written like that because the accent falls on the second note. The first note is called the **upbeat**, because that's literally how a conductor would conduct it, leading into the first beat of the bar, which is always a downbeat.

If you think of a few well-known tunes, you may be able to sense whether they start on the first beat of the bar, with an accented note, or on an upbeat, leading into an accented note.

For instance, think of the National Anthem:

> **God** save our **gra**-cious queen.

It starts on the first beat of the bar. Now think of *Auld Lang Syne*:

> Should **auld** acquaintance **be** forgot.

'Should' is an upbeat, and 'auld' falls on the first beat of the first full bar.

RECOGNISING TUNES

Here's a real test; don't worry if you find it difficult. It involves reading the rhythm *and* reading how the pitch changes. Try approaching it like this:

1 Look at the time signature. How many beats are there in each bar?

2 Count steadily, paying some attention to the tempo mark.

3 Try to work out the rhythm, and how it fits against the steady beat.

4 Go through the rhythm again, but imagining the notes going up or down (or staying the same), according to how they appear on the stave.

Now, using that method, look carefully at this example. Can you work out what it is?

Andante (walking pace)

Have you got the answer? If you can't get it, look at the answer on page 126. Then look at the notation again.

◆ Can you make sense of the rhythm as written? (Which beats fall *between* the notes of the tune?)

◆ Following the rise and fall of the tune, can you hear that mostly it moves up or down to a next-door note, but twice it moves up or down by a larger gap?

◆ Listening to the tune in your head, can you hear how it comes back to the first note? As you listen (or sing to yourself), follow it on the stave.

Two more tunes to identify

First this one:

And now this one:

Did you manage to identify either of those tunes? Don't worry if you found it too difficult: look at the answers on page 126, then (if you know how the tunes go) try to match them to the notation, seeing how the rhythms and the visible rise and fall of the notes match how the tune sounds.

REFLECTING ON YOUR PROGRESS

This is a good time to think about how much you have achieved so far.

'Reading music', in the sense of hearing it in your head, is not easy, at least for most of us. That's not really what this book is about. On the other hand, you now understand the essence of music notation: pitch and rhythm. Everything else is an elaboration – even though there are some quite important elaborations still to cover. If you look now at some printed music you will probably find plenty of symbols that you don't understand. We'll try to deal with them (or as many of them as possible) in the rest of this book.

TWO NOTES AT A TIME

Two instruments

So far we have only dealt with one note at a time. Yet much music involves several sounds at the same time, and this is visible in the notation. Here, for instance, is some music for two flutes:

At the left-hand end of each line of music you can see a vertical line, joining two staves together. This shows that the two instruments play together. The barlines are aligned vertically, and so are the notes. The beat that runs through the music (at three crotchet beats per bar) applies to both staves simultaneously, and is what keeps the two instruments synchronised.

Two instruments, different rhythms

The same is still true even if the two flutes play different rhythms. The *beat* and the *barlines* still coincide:

Piano music

Piano music uses two staves for one instrument – generally the treble clef for the right hand and the bass clef for the left, though that's not a strict rule. Of course, each hand can play several notes simultaneously, so piano music can look very busy. Here is a single chord for piano. The left hand plays the C and G below middle C. The right hand plays the E, G and C above middle C. The notes are aligned vertically, so all five notes should be played exactly together. The curved bracket at the beginning conventionally joins the left- and right-hand staves in piano music.

How many notes are there in the next example?

Two? Well actually it's one, because they're both middle C; both hands are asked to play the same note. That looks silly, because you don't need both hands to play it. But in practice there are times when it makes sense to use this sort of notation. For instance, look at this:

There's a short tune in the right hand (the top stave), accompanied by a bass-line in the left hand (bottom stave). Both 'parts' end on the same note – again, it happens to be middle C, though it could equally be another note. In this case it makes sense to write the final note in both staves, because really it belongs to both the melody and the bass-line.

Music in two or more 'parts'

We can talk about music being in several **parts** or **voices**, meaning different lines or tunes happening at the same time. They may be played by different instruments, or sung by different singers, but on piano or keyboard – and also on other instruments such as harp or guitar – it is possible for the one instrument to play several parts.

POINTS TO REMEMBER

1 **Note-values**, together with the **time signature**, tell you about **rhythm**. The **position of notes on the stave**, together with the **clef**, tell you about pitch.

2 **Note-stems** can go up or down. It makes no difference to the note-value or the pitch.

3 A tune or piece of music may begin on the first beat of the bar. Equally, though, it may begin on a different beat.

4 If it begins on the last beat of the bar, that beat is called the **upbeat**.

5 If you're trying to recognise a tune from notation, the first things to look at are the time signature and rhythm.

6 Two instruments playing together are written on two staves, joined together at the left-hand end by a vertical line.

7 When instruments are playing together, the barlines and beats are aligned vertically. Notes played at the same time are also aligned vertically.

8 Piano music is written on two staves, normally with a treble clef for the right hand and a bass clef for the left hand, and with a curved bracket joining the two staves.

9 When music has several different lines or tunes happening at the same time, these are called **parts** or **voices**.

5

Sharps and Flats

In the course of this chapter we'll work our way through two important areas:

◆ sharps and flats

◆ tones and semitones.

They are closely related.

SO WHAT ABOUT THE BLACK NOTES?

To start with, let's remind ourselves how the notes on the treble stave relate to the white notes on a piano keyboard.

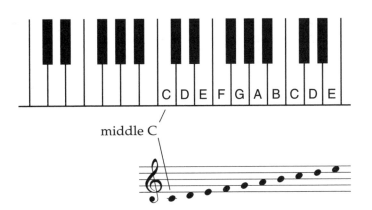

So where do the black notes fit in? What letter-names do they have?

Listening to the black and white notes

If possible, get access to a piano or keyboard. Starting on C (any C), play every note upwards (rightwards) for one octave, i.e. as far as the next C. Play the black *and* white notes, like this:

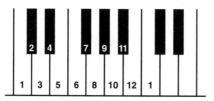

Twelve notes in the octave

After twelve notes you reach the next C. Thus there are twelve steps from one C to the next, provided you play the black notes as well as the white notes.

TONES AND SEMITONES

Some important concepts are coming up:

◆ These twelve steps are *equal* – i.e. the octave is divided into *twelve equal portions*.

◆ These steps or portions are called **semitones**.

◆ Two semitones equals one **tone**.

Understanding tones and semitones

Look at the following statements, and make sure you understand them:

◆ There are twelve semitones in each octave.

◆ There are six tones in each octave.

◆ This is true of *any* octave, whichever note you start on.

◆ An octave is like a ladder with 13 equally spaced rungs (making 12 equal gaps).

Tones and semitones on the piano

The idea that an octave has twelve equal semitone gaps contrasts rather oddly with the irregular pattern of the black notes on a piano keyboard.

Any two adjacent notes on the piano – irrespective of whether black or white – are a semitone apart. But 'adjacent' is meant strictly; two white notes are not adjacent if they have a black note in between, but *are* adjacent if there is no black note in between.

Therefore *some* of the white notes are a semitone apart, but others are a tone apart.

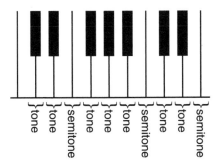

That may seem surprising, but once again it helps if you can hear the difference. So if you have access to a keyboard, play from C up to the next C playing all the notes, white and black. Then play from C to C again, this time playing only the white notes.

A sequence of notes like that, rising or falling, is called a **scale**.

Can you hear the difference between the tones and semitones? It doesn't necessarily sound that big a difference – but the tones are bigger gaps than the semitones. Twice as big, in fact.

SCALES

The chromatic scale

Once again, play from C to C, *all* the notes, white and black. This scale is called the **chromatic** scale. It consists entirely of semitones.

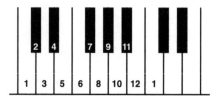

The major scale

Now, as you did before, play from C to C playing *only the white notes.*

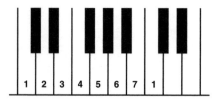

This scale has a mixture of tones and semitones. Listen again, if possible – and perhaps sing along. Can you *hear* that the step from E to F is smaller than the step from F to G, and similarly that B to C is a smaller step than A to B?

Those are the two semitone steps – E/F and B/C. When you play up (or down) the white notes, all the other steps are tones.

Play again from C to C, white notes only. This scale has a very familiar ring; it is the **major scale**. We can write it down, without any rhythm, like this:

C   D   E   F   G   A   B   C

The steps from one note to another look equal from the way they are written on the stave. But now you know the steps are not equal; from E to F and from B to C are semitones, but the other steps are tones.

Tones and semitones in the major scale

What makes the major scale distinctive and familiar is its pattern of tones and semitones:

tone   tone   semitone   tone   tone   tone   semitone

Check this pattern against the notation and against the keyboard diagram.

The white notes are called by letter-names from A to G. What then are the black notes called?

SHARPS AND FLATS

Yes, that's what they're called. And *each* black note can be named as a sharp or a flat, relative to the white note on either side.

For instance, the black note between C and D is called **C sharp** (C♯) or **D flat** (D♭).

Sharp and flat signs

The sharp or flat sign can be placed immediately in front of a note on the stave. Here, for instance is middle C:

And here is C sharp, the black note immediately above middle C:

And here is D flat, which is exactly the same note:

Or, of course, it could be written in the bass clef:

Similarly, F♯ is the black note just above (to the right of) F, and B♭ is the black note just below (to the left of) B. Here are four F♯s and four B♭s:

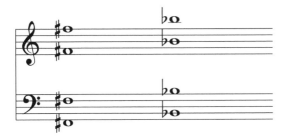

CONFUSINGLY, ANOTHER (RELATED) MEANING FOR 'SHARP' AND 'FLAT'

We have examined the way the black notes on a piano keyboard are named 'sharp' or 'flat' in relation to the adjacent white notes. The semitone that lies between F and G is F♯ or G♭.

However, the words 'sharp' and 'flat' are sometimes used in a more general way, to mean 'above pitch' (sharp) or 'below pitch' (flat). Typically, that would mean *relative to the correct pitch* – for instance, if you are in a choir, and the conductor complains that you are singing too sharp or too flat.

But we're concentrating on notation here, so the more precise meaning is the one that matters to us; there isn't normally any real danger of confusing the two.

Away from the piano

What about other instruments? We refer to the piano because it is a useful *visual* way of understanding the layout of the tones and semitones within the octave. Musically that layout is always the same, irrespective of instrument. F and G are *always* a tone apart, and the semitone in between can be described as F♯ or G♭.

TEST YOURSELF

Before we go on, would you like to test your understanding and knowledge of tones and semitones, sharps and flats?

Are these two notes a tone or semitone apart?

Here are some more pairs. For each pair, decide whether the notes are a tone or semitone apart. Don't forget to look at the clef.

Now put a name to each of these notes:

Finally, here are some more difficult pairs. Are they a tone or semitone apart? Answers are on pages 126–7.

POINTS TO REMEMBER

1 The **octave** is divided into twelve equal **semitones**.

2 Two semitones equals one **tone**.

3 On a piano, C to D is one tone, and so is D to E. But E to F is a semitone, because there is no black note in between. Similarly, B to C is a semitone.

4 A scale is a sequence of notes arranged in rising or falling order.

5 A **chromatic scale** consists entirely of semitones.

6 A **major scale** has a mixture of tones and semitones.

7 The black notes on a piano are **sharps** or **flats**.

8 The black note between C and D is called **C sharp** if it is written as a C with a sharp sign in front of it. But it is called **D flat** if it is written as a D with a flat sign in front of it.

9 The terms 'sharp' and 'flat' are also used more generally, to mean 'above pitch' (sharp) or 'below pitch' (flat).

6

Scales

WRITING OUT THE CHROMATIC SCALE

Consider again the **chromatic scale**, the one which includes all the semitones. Now we can write it down in notation:

We could have used flats instead, or a mixture of sharps and flats. But there's a general tendency to use sharps when the melody is rising and flats when it's falling.

We can start a chromatic scale on any note, even a black note. It'll sound much the same (apart from being higher or lower), because it consists entirely of semitones from top to bottom.

WRITING OUT THE MAJOR SCALE

The order of tones and semitones

The **major scale**, however, has to be approached more carefully. When we encountered it in the last chapter, it took the form of all the white notes from C to C. But if we try to start it on a different note – say D – and play all the white notes again, we get a different effect, because the pattern of tones and semitones has been changed.

All major scales follow this pattern:

tone   tone   semitone   tone   tone   tone   semitone

At this point it is helpful once again to look at the keyboard diagram. Let's start on D, and mark out the steps of the major scale:

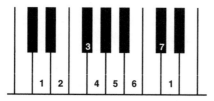

The *first* step in the scale, which must be a tone, takes us from D to E. But the *second* step – *also* a tone (see the list of tones and semitones at the top of the page) – doesn't take us from E to F, which would be a semitone, but from E to F♯.

Let's check all the steps shown on the keyboard diagram:

From D to E: **tone**

From E to F♯: **tone**

From F♯ to G: **semitone**

From G to A: **tone**

From A to B: **tone**

From B to C♯: **tone**

From C♯ to D: **semitone**

That's a major scale; it matches the list of tones and semitones at the top of the page. If you have some way of playing that sequence of notes, with the F♯ and C♯ in place of F and C, it should sound correct as a major scale.

Writing out the D major scale

Now that we've definitely got the right sequence of tones and semitones, we can look at that scale – the **D major scale** – in notation:

Can you see how it matches the keyboard diagram on the previous page? And can you see why we need to play F♯ and C♯ in place of F and C in order to preserve the order of tones and semitones that makes the major scale?

THE F MAJOR SCALE

Working out the notes

Scales are generally important to musicians, and major scales particularly so. I hope they don't seem too complex – or for that matter too boring – because we need to spend some more time on them yet.

In the D major scale we used F♯ and C♯ in place of F and C in order to get the correct sequence of tones and semitones. Let's look now at another major scale, this time starting on F:

first step	**tone**	F to G
second step	**tone**	G to A
third step	**semitone**	A to ...?

A to B would be a tone; we must choose the black note *below* B, i.e. B♭.

When to use sharps and when to use flats

We *could* call that note A♯, but because we're using it instead of B, B♭ is preferred. A black note is thought of as a sharp if it is used in place of the white note below, or as a flat if it replaces the white note above.

Now we can continue with the F major scale, completing our list of steps:

third step	**semitone**	A to B♭
fourth step	**tone**	B♭ to C
fifth step	**tone**	C to D
sixth step	**tone**	D to E
seventh step	**semitone**	E to F

So the scale of F major uses just one black note, B♭. Written out, it will look like this:

THE STRANGE CASE OF E SHARP

The black notes on a piano, we learnt at the beginning of the last chapter, are named as sharps or flats. So does that mean that *all* sharps or flats, if played on a piano, are black notes? Strangely enough, no.

Consider this. The black note below E is E♭. But since there is no black note *above* E, does that mean there is no E♯? No it doesn't; there *is* an E♯, and, yes, it's the same as F.

So why would we need E♯, why not just use F?

Here's why. We can play a major scale starting on any note, including black notes. Let's start on F♯. First we must go through the process of adding steps in the correct order of tones or semitones. Remember the order?

tone   tone   semitone   tone   tone   tone   semitone

Applying that process, we get the following sequence of notes:

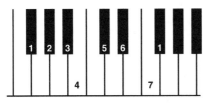

Can you see that provided we start on F♯, those are the notes we play in order to get a scale of F♯ major?

Now let's think about how those notes are named. Notes 1–6 are F♯, G♯, A♯, B, C♯ and D♯. That much is straightforward.

But note 7 is more accurately described as E♯ than F, since it is a sharpened note in lieu of E (just as we used C♯ in place of C in order to get a correct scale of D major, on page 53). Look at it in notation:

It would be 'wrong' – *in this context* – to use F in place of E♯.

Another view of the same scale

A similar argument would apply if we were to describe this scale as
Gb major rather than F♯ major. Note 7 would then be F, coming
between Eb and Gb. Note 4, however, would be Cb rather than B,
coming between Bb and Db.

Look at those two scales, and check that you're happy to agree that
they describe exactly the same notes. Look at one of the keyboard
diagrams if you're not sure.

These justifications for describing even white notes as sharps or
flats may seem abstruse. The important thing is to realise that there
can be a Cb – and if you see one, there's probably a good reason for
calling it Cb even though it's the same note as B.

POINTS TO REMEMBER

1 All major scales follow the same pattern of tones and
   semitones.

2 Basing a major scale on a different starting note results in
   different needs for sharps or flats.

3 When a sharp or flat is needed in a scale, it is thought of as a
   sharp if it replaces the white note below, or as a flat if it
   replaces the white note above.

7

Keys

WHY ARE SCALES SO IMPORTANT?

Most good musicians have spent a great deal of time practising scales, especially major scales.

Partly this is because it's a good way of becoming acquainted with one's instrument. On the piano, every major scale has a different layout of black and white notes. On a wind instrument it will be different holes to cover or valves to open, together with control of the 'embouchure' (mouth shape). On a string instrument it's the fingering involved in pressing down the right string at the right point. Playing scales, on *any* instrument, is a route to fluency, enabling the fingers to learn habits of melodic playing.

Scales and keys

But there's another reason why major scales are specially important. The major scale is the musical basis on which a huge amount of music is built. You will have heard the phrase **'in the key of...'**, or of a symphony being (for instance) **'in C'** or **'in C major'** – or indeed **'in C minor'**, but we'll come to minor keys later.

UNDERSTANDING KEYS

This whole subject of **keys** links closely to scales. Consider the tune 'Twinkle twinkle little star' – just the first two lines of the rhyme:

Twin-kle twin-kle lit - tle star,   How I won-der what you are.

It uses most of the notes of a C major scale – all but the B. C is the first note and the last note, and if you play it you may agree that there is some sense of C being the 'home' note, the note at which the tune is 'at rest'. This is called the **keynote**.

Changing the starting note

Just as we can start a major scale on any note, similarly we can start a simple tune like 'Twinkle twinkle' on any note. We have seen it **in the key of** C major (or simply 'in C major'); now here is the tune in the key of F major:

Note the B♭. As with scales, the character of the tune depends on preserving the same melodic shape, whatever the starting note, and in this case we need the step down from 'star' to 'How' to be a tone, not a semitone.

Incidentally, the second B in bar 3 is also B♭. A sharp or flat sign placed in front of a note then continues to apply *as far as the next barline*.

The role of sharps and flats

It's not surprising that when we put 'Twinkle twinkle' into the key of F major the tune uses B♭ instead of B. We have seen that exactly the same is true of the *scale* of F major (pages 57–58).

Any tune in the *key* of F major will consist predominantly of the notes of the *scale* of F major, including B♭s. Similarly, any tune in D major will be based on the notes of the D major scale, including F♯ and C♯.

KEY SIGNATURES

To avoid plastering scores with large numbers of sharp signs and flat signs, we use **key signatures**. A key signature consists of one or more sharp or flat signs written *at the beginning of every stave*, just after the clef. It means play those sharps or flats *throughout*.

Here is the scale of D major once more, this time written with its key signature:

The F♯ in the key signature is written on the top line of the stave, not the bottom space, but it means play *all* Fs as F♯s, not just at that octave but at any octave.

'Twinkle twinkle' in various keys

Now let's see 'Twinkle twinkle' in the key of D major, and written with a key signature – the same key signature as the scale, of course.

The Fs in bar 3 are played as F♯. There's no C in this tune – but if there were the key signature would turn it into C♯.

Here is 'Twinkle twinkle' again, this time in F major:

You will hardly need to be told that the first two notes of bar 3 are both B♭.

Next, here is 'Twinkle twinkle' in F♯ major:

The key signature takes care of the sharps or flats each time.

KEY SIGNATURES IN THE BASS CLEF

Key signatures look just the same in the bass clef, but of course adjusted to be on the right lines or spaces. Here is the key signature for D major, set out on treble and bass clefs, as if for piano music:

And here is the key signature for F major:

TEST YOURSELF

This is quite an elaborate test. If you have access to a piano or keyboard, use it; otherwise use a keyboard diagram to help you.

1   Start on E, the E above middle C.

2   What are the notes of the major scale starting on E? Start by reminding yourself of the correct sequence of tones and semitones. (Look back at Chapter 6 for this.) Work out the notes of the scale one by one, writing out a list as you go.

3   How many sharps or flats did you need? Which ones? Provided you got the right answer, *that* will be the key signature for E major. (Answer on page 127.)

4   If you feel like trying to write out some music, try writing out the scale of E major, in the treble clef. Use some manuscript paper, or simply rule yourself five lines on a blank sheet of paper. You can put the sharp or flat signs in front of the notes, or at the beginning of the stave as a key signature.

ALL THE KEY SIGNATURES

Each major key or scale has its own key signature. Here they all are (below and continuing onto the next page), shown on the treble clef:

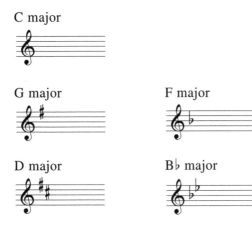

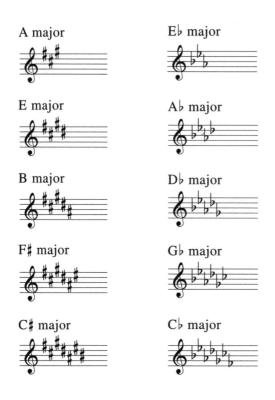

A major

E major

B major

F♯ major

C♯ major

E♭ major

A♭ major

D♭ major

G♭ major

C♭ major

Why are there fifteen key signatures here, when there are only twelve different notes in the octave? For an answer, look closely at the bottom six: any duplications?

How key signatures are arranged on the stave

Remembering that a key signature affects notes at *all* octaves, does it matter how key signatures are arranged on the stave?

Actually it does – even though the way key signatures are written is purely a matter of convention. F♯ is always written on the top line of the treble clef, not the bottom space, and G♯ always on the space just above the stave, not the second line up as one might expect. The *order* of sharps or flats in a key signature is also always the same.

Why? The answer is that performers, when they are playing from a printed copy, need to take in a huge amount of information at high speed – including possibly a change of key signature which must be grasped in a single glance, a fraction of a second. Musicians are used to absorbing that information without even thinking about it, and an unconventionally written key signature would confuse the eye, creating alarm. Trying to play the right notes gives them enough to worry about, without puzzling over strange-looking key signatures.

Key signatures in the bass clef also follow a set pattern, much like the treble clef and using the same order: see the examples on page 64.

TEST YOURSELF AGAIN

Here are six key signatures. Three of them are correctly set out, three incorrectly. Which are correct, and which major keys do they signify? Which are the three incorrect ones? Answers on page 127.

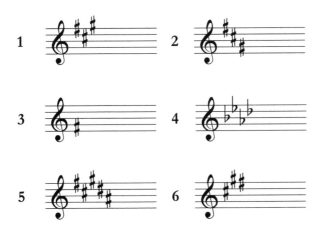

POINTS TO REMEMBER

1 Tunes, like scales, can start on different notes – but like scales will then need different sharps or flats in order to 'sound right'.

2 The sharps or flats needed form a **key signature** which is placed at the beginning of each stave, just after the clef.

3 A key signature tells anyone looking at the score that the notes indicated, at any octave, should be sharpened or flattened (as indicated), throughout the piece.

4 The bottom note of a major scale is called the **keynote**, and that note is also the keynote of a tune or piece which is in that key. When you are listening, the keynote 'feels' like the 'home' or most important note; it may well be the final note, though not necessarily.

5 Every major key has a different key signature.

6 Each key signature is always written out in the same way, with the sharps or flats always in the same order.

8

Major and Minor

As well as major scales there are...

MINOR SCALES

Vive la différence

Like the major scale, what distinguishes a minor scale is its particular sequence of tones and semitones. However, it's not so easy to say exactly what this sequence is, for two reasons:

1   There is more than one type of minor scale.

2   One of these types varies between its ascending and descending forms.

We needn't explore these complications fully here. But we should at least look at the first five notes (which are the same for *all* types of minor scale).

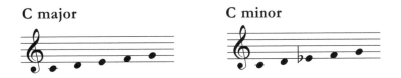

As you can see, it's the third note that's different. If you have access to an instrument, play the two examples. The difference in sound is the essential difference between major and minor.

In a minor scale, the third note is a semitone flatter than in a major scale. In a tune in a minor key, that note on the third degree of the scale has a big influence; that's what gives it the minor key sound.

Relating major and minor

There is a relationship between major and minor keys. For every major key there is a minor key with the same key signature. They are called **relative** major and minor.

The *sixth* note of a major scale is the keynote of its relative minor. For instance, D minor is the relative minor of F major. Both keys have a key signature of one flat (B♭ – check the table of major key signatures on page 65).

Minor tunes

There are tunes in minor keys just as there are tunes in major keys. Any minor tune probably has mainly the same notes as its corresponding minor *scale*, with the same keynote and the same flattened third degree of the scale.

Distinguishing minor tunes from major tunes

For a start, you can't distinguish minor from major just from the key signature. For every key signature there is a major key and a relative minor key. How then can we tell which key a tune is in, from looking at the score?

The key signature is still important of course, but one has to look at the notes as well. Look at these two tunes, which both have a key signature of one flat. Can you recognise either of them, by looking at the melodic contour and at the rhythms? (Answers on page 127.)

1

How can we tell what key they're in? From the key signature it must be F major or D minor. There is no absolute, exact way of telling which it is, but in practice the melody usually offers some strong clues.

Look at the first tune. It starts on F, ends on F, has lots of Fs, and (as it happens) no Ds at all. That isn't exactly proof, but it's a strong indication.

Now look at the second tune. This starts on D, ends on D and keeps returning to D. In fact it starts with the first five notes of the D minor scale. Once again, strongly indicative.

If you can, play these two tunes. Or, if you have worked out what they are, can you hear them in your head? Can you *hear* that one is major and the other minor? Following the printed music, can you hear that F is the keynote of the first tune, its 'home' note, and that D is the keynote of the second tune? Try playing, or singing to yourself, the first five notes of the F major scale, and then of the D minor scale.

However, it's not always so easy to tell the key. Don't assume that a tune starts or finishes on its keynote; it may not. And a long piece of music may not stay in one key; in fact it may change key several times. More about that soon.

HOW KEYS CONTRIBUTE TO MUSICAL STRUCTURE

When we consider what key a piece of music is in, we're beginning to move away from our main purpose – how music is notated – towards the larger issue of how music is constructed.

Yet, to be able to read music you have to know something about keys, to make sense of the key signatures. Anyone who learns an instrument learns to play scales in different keys, and we have seen here how a simple tune can be printed in different keys. Knowledge of keys is essential for a performer and useful also to a listener.

On a basic level, the important thing is to realise that most music is *in a key* of some sort, and that there is a *keynote* or home note, a note which represents a sort of melodic resting-place. This is true for most kinds of music.

Modulation

When we're in C major, other closely-related keys are G major (with a key signature of one sharp) and F major (one flat). Another closely-related key is the *relative minor*, A minor. By contrast, keys such as B major (five sharps) or D♭ major (five flats) are considered distant keys from C major. A classical minuet in C major might **modulate** (change key) to G major in the middle, and then modulate back to C major before the end. A sonata, however, may modulate several times, perhaps reaching quite distant keys, before eventually returning to its home key. Listening actively to a piece of music is like undertaking a journey; what happens by way of key-changes can be an important part of the changing landscape.

Changing the key signature

It is quite possible to change key signature in the middle of a piece. Here's a skeleton score – some empty bars – to show what it can look like. The double barline helps draw attention to the change.

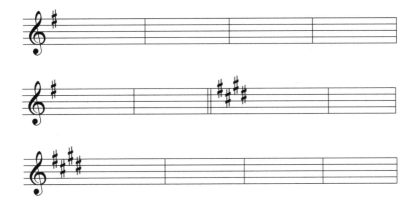

However, if the music changes key very briefly – just for a few bars – then it may be notated without a change of key signature. Instead, the notes will be marked individually with sharp or flat signs, as necessary. Here is a passage which starts in G major but moves into D major. The F♯ is in the key signature while the extra C♯ is marked individually.

ACCIDENTALS

When sharps or flats are marked at the beginning of a line, they form, as you know, a *key signature*. They then apply to all occurrences of those notes, at any octave and throughout the piece (or until contradicted by a change of key signature).

However, when sharps or flats are marked next to the note they are called **accidentals**. They then apply *only at the octave marked*, not to the same note an octave above or below. They apply *to the note marked, and to any subsequent occurrence of that note within the same bar*. In other words, the effect of the accidental lasts up to the next barline, but no further.

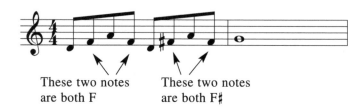

These two notes
are both F

These two notes
are both F♯

NATURALS

As well as sharps and flats, there is a third type of accidental you need to know about: **naturals**. A natural sign looks like this:

♮

and its effect is to *cancel* a sharp or flat – either one which would otherwise apply because of the key signature, or an accidental occurring earlier in the same bar.

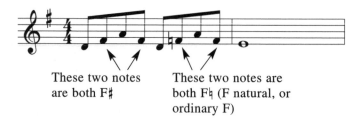

These two notes
are both F♯

These two notes are
both F♮ (F natural, or
ordinary F)

ACCIDENTALS IN ACTION

Accidentals don't necessarily indicate a change of key, a *modulation*. Even though a tune is in a certain key, it may include notes that aren't part of that scale. This theme is from a fugue by Bach in F minor, but it uses plenty of accidentals as you can see:

Now another fragment of Bach (from a prelude in B minor):

What's that natural sign doing in bar 3? Surely the note is G natural anyway, since the sharp sign in the previous bar only operates up to the barline?

Absolutely correct. But in practice a performer might easily play another G sharp by mistake at this point, so the natural sign is helpful as a prompt, even though it is not strictly required. Such prompts are sometimes called **courtesy accidentals** or **cautionary accidentals**. In modern or complex music, it is advisable to be generous with cautionary accidentals; performers prefer it, and often end up writing their own into the score, to avoid mistakes.

POINTS TO REMEMBER

1 The third note of a minor scale is a semitone flatter than the third note of a major scale.

2 Each major key has a **relative** minor key. The sixth note of a major scale is the keynote of its relative minor.

3 Relative major and minor keys share the same key signature.

4 To **modulate** is to change key.

5 Sharps or flats can form a key signature, or they can be placed directly in front of a note, in which case they are called **accidentals**. An accidental applies as far as the next barline.

6 The sharps or flats forming a key signature apply at every octave, but accidentals only apply to the pitch at which they are marked.

7 A **natural** is an accidental which cancels a sharp or flat.

8 **Cautionary** or **courtesy** accidentals are not strictly necessary, but are widely used as reminders to help performers avoid mistakes.

9

Rhythm Round-up

In this chapter we will look at several important notational matters which we have not mentioned up to now, all to do with *rhythm* or *duration*.

TIES

A **tie** is a curved line. It joins two note-values to be played as a single note. It may be used:

1   if the combined note-value cannot be expressed as a single note:

2   if the combined long note goes across a barline:

3   if the combined long note goes across the beginning of a beat, and the overall pattern of beats is easier for the eye to take in when a tie is used:

Ties and accidentals

If a tied note is modified by an accidental, the accidental doesn't need to be repeated at the right-hand end of the tie, even if the tie goes across a barline:

This is still G♯

But if a further G♯ is wanted in that second bar, then the accidental must be marked:

Multiple ties

Ties can be strung together, and long notes lasting many bars are not uncommon. Here is a long horn note from Beethoven's Fifth Symphony:

Also, of course, simultaneous notes can be tied:

It matters not whether the curve goes up or down. As with note-stems, it generally depends on whether the note-head is in the top or bottom half of the stave. The examples printed here show typical practice.

SLURS

Ties should not be confused with **slurs** (or **phrase marks**). These look very similar – also curved lines – but join notes of *different* pitches. Here is a flute phrase from the same symphony, Beethoven's Fifth. (In fact it happens during the long horn note.)

These are not ties. Ties always join notes of the *same* pitch, and one tie only ever joins two notes, not more. More about slurs and phrase marks later. They don't really belong in this chapter, because they're not to do with duration, but are mentioned here because it's important to distinguish them from ties.

RESTS

Do you remember the note-values and their names?

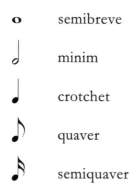

semibreve

minim

crotchet

quaver

semiquaver

As well as playing notes, performers must sometimes leave gaps between notes – timed gaps, which relate to the steady ticking beat just as precisely as the notes do. These gaps need to be notated, just like the notes, and this is done with **rests** – the silent equivalent of the notes.

semibreve rest (shown on the stave)

minim rest (shown on the stave)

crotchet rest

quaver rest

semiquaver rest

The semibreve rest always hangs from one of the stave lines (normally the fourth line up). The minim rest always sits on one of the stave lines (normally the third line).

Dotted rests

Rests can be dotted, just like notes, to make them one-and-a-half times as long.

dotted minim rest

 dotted crotchet rest

dotted quaver rest

Whole-bar rests

The semibreve rest, somewhat confusingly, is also used to signify a whole-bar rest whatever the time signature. In other words, in 3/4 time, a whole-bar rest is shown like this:

and not like this:

Multi-bar rests

One other sign you may see is this:

(Or with a different numeral.) That means 12 bars rest. This style of multi-bar rest usually occurs on an instrumental part, when that instrument has to wait for a number of bars while others are playing.

MORE ABOUT TIME SIGNATURES

Revising the basics

You have learnt that in a time signature, the top figure indicates the number of beats per bar while the bottom figure indicates what kind of beats they are.

There are exceptions to that pattern, as we will now find out.

Six-eight time

In 6/8 time there are not 6 beats but 2. Each beat is a *dotted crotchet* – worth three quavers. So there *are* six quavers in each bar, but grouped in two lots of three.

9/8 and 12/8 time, similarly, have dotted crotchet beats, each of which sub-divides into three quavers. In 9/8 time there are three beats per bar, and in 12/8 there are four beats per bar.

Counting in six-eight

To count in 6/8, start by counting the six quavers, quite fast:

1 2 3 4 5 6 **1** 2 3 4 5 6

Then give a big emphasis to the **1** and a smaller emphasis to the **4**:

<u>**1**</u> 2 3 <u>**4**</u> 5 6 <u>**1**</u> 2 3 <u>**4**</u> 5 6

Next, just count the two beats per bar, but stay aware of the quavers, so that you can hear in your head how each beat subdivides into three.

Distinguishing six-eight from three-four

Can you see the difference between 6/8 time and 3/4 time, which also has six quavers in each bar? In 3/4 the quavers are grouped in 3 lots of 2, i.e. three crotchet beats per bar. In 6/8 the quavers are grouped in 2 lots of 3, i.e. two dotted crotchet beats per bar.

This distinction is often clear from the way the quavers are **beamed**. There is no absolute rule about how quavers and semiquavers should be beamed – it depends on the detailed circumstances – but generally it is done in a way that reflects the time signature, making it easy for the eye to grasp the beat structure.

Six-eight in action

Here's the start of a tune in 6/8 time. It has a skipping rhythm very characteristic of this time signature.

POINTS TO REMEMBER

1 A **tie** joins two note-values to be played as a single note.

2 Ties always join notes of the same pitch, whereas **slurs**, which look similar, normally join notes of different pitches.

3 If a tied note is modified by an accidental, the accidental need not be written again at the right-hand end of the tie.

4 A tie appears as a curved line between (not quite touching) the two note-heads. The curve can be up or down; it makes no difference.

5 **Rests** are the silent equivalent of notes. There is a rest for each note-value. Rests are used where silences are required within the music.

6 Rests can be dotted in just the same way as notes.

7 The **semibreve rest** is also used as a **whole-bar rest**.

8 In **6/8 time** there are two beats, each worth a dotted crotchet. Therefore there are six quavers per bar, divided into two lots of three.

10

Chords

MEASURING FROM ONE NOTE TO ANOTHER

The distance from one note to another is called an **interval**. Here
are some intervals, and the names used to describe them:

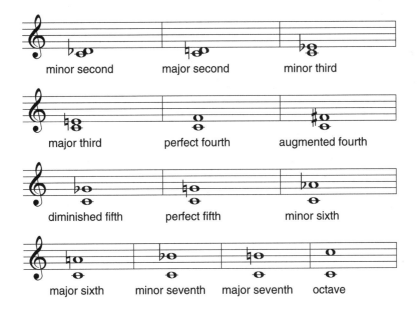

As you see, the intervals are presented here in gradually widening
order.

- a **minor second** = one semitone

- a **major second** = two semitones or one tone

- a **minor third** = three semitones

and so on.

Look closely at the **augmented fourth** and the **diminished fifth**. They are the same interval (because F♯ is the same as G♭) – both six semitones. The choice of interval-name will correspond to the choice of note-name, so that in this case, for instance, C to G♭ is correctly described as a diminished fifth, but C to F♯ is correctly described as an augmented fourth.

How intervals are described

The list on the previous page is not comprehensive; there are other intervals. For example, from C to D♯ is an **augmented second**. But you can see a pattern: irrespective of sharps, flats or naturals, Cs to Ds are always *seconds* of some sort, Cs to Es are *thirds*, Cs to Fs are *fourths*, and so on.

This may seem a bit puzzling: after all, Cs and Ds are one note apart, Cs and Es two notes apart, and Cs and Fs three notes apart. But that's the way intervals are numbered, and we have to accept it. Just remember that intervals count both the top and the bottom note: C–D–E, therefore C to E is a *third*.

When we get to an *eighth*, we meet an old friend: the *octave*.

Intervals and scales

A scale is a succession of *notes*, but you can also regard it as a succession of *intervals*. We have already seen how the major scale has a unique order of tones and semitones that makes it what it is.

Intervals and chords

In the same way, when notes are played simultaneously they make combinations of intervals. And particular combinations of intervals make particular chords.

MAJOR CHORDS

This is a **C major chord**. It consists of a *major third* (from C to E) plus a *minor third* (from E to G) – or you can look at it as a *major third* (C to E) plus a *perfect fifth* (C to G).

Other versions of the C major chord

If any of the notes is moved up or down by an octave (or several octaves), the chord is still a C major chord. Also, notes may be **doubled** – included a second time at a different octave. The chords below are all different versions of C major; they all consist of C, E and G.

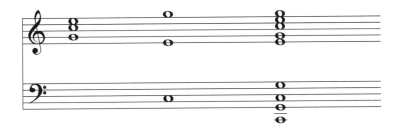

Transposing

If you take a C major chord and **transpose** it – shift it up or down, but without changing the relationships between the notes – you get another major chord.

It's just the same as when you start a major scale on a different note, but keep the correct order of tones and semitones.

MINOR AND OTHER CHORDS

Once you change the *intervals*, however – not just by moving notes up or down an octave, but actually changing one of the notes – you get a completely different chord. For instance:

This is a **D minor chord**. The lowest interval, from D to F, is a *minor third*, and you may notice that this chord consists of the first, third and fifth notes of the D minor scale, just as a major chord consists of the first, third and fifth notes of its corresponding *major* scale – as you can see from any of the examples above.

Keys, scales and chords, as you can see, are closely bound together.

Why are chords important?

Along with *melody* and *rhythm*, chords make the third ingredient of music: **harmony**.

It is perfectly possible to have music without harmony. Most folk-song, in its original form, has melody *without* chords, as does religious plainsong, and the melodic music of many cultures around the world. However, adding harmony is one way of giving music a sense of forward propulsion, and for most types of popular music, as well as Western classical music, harmony is a vital structural element. And the simplest way of adding harmony is through a series of different chords accompanying a melody.

The choice of chords will relate to the key the melody is in. Major and minor chords are the most common, but there are many other types of chords with names to identify them, as well as other possible chords too obscure to have generic names.

CHORD SYMBOLS

Chords can be notated in full, note by note. However, you may also see a melody – probably a vocal line – with **chord symbols** written above the notes, for instance like this:

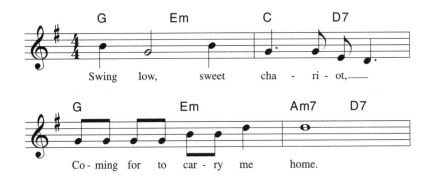

These chord symbols are not instrument-specific – but are usually thought of as being for guitar or keyboard. Pop songs are sometimes printed with small guitar-chord diagrams beside the chord symbols. The diagrams show where the left hand presses on the frets to obtain the notes of that chord.

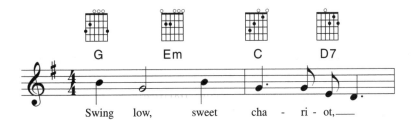

The language of chord symbols

Chord symbols are a form of shorthand.

C	means C major
Cm	means C minor
C7	means 'C seven' – a C major chord with a minor seventh (from the C) added
Cm7	means 'C minor seven' – a C minor chord with the minor seventh added.

There are many other kinds of chords (including other kinds of seventh chords), with their own names and chord symbols. A chord is a combination of two or more notes played simultaneously, and many different combinations of notes are possible. But the types we have looked at – major, minor and seventh chords – are the most common ones.

POINTS TO REMEMBER

1 An **interval** is the distance from one note to another.

2 Intervals are measured in a way that counts both the bottom and top notes. For instance, from C to E is a *third*.

3 A **C major chord** has the notes C, E and G. From C to E is a *major third* and from C to G is a *perfect fifth*. Other major chords, though **transposed** to different notes, use exactly the same intervals.

4 Major chords contain the first, third and fifth notes of the corresponding major scale. Likewise, minor chords contain the first, third and fifth notes of the corresponding minor scale.

5 **Chord symbols** are a shorthand alternative to writing out the chord.

11

Odds and Ends

Basically you have covered the essence of reading music – well done! In this chapter we will go through a few miscellaneous matters that haven't fitted in elsewhere: repeat marks, expression marks and a few other things. Then in the final chapter we can look at a few examples of music notation in action.

Let's just remind ourselves of the areas covered so far:

◆   pitch, note-names

◆   rhythm, note-values, time signatures

◆   keys, scales, chord-names, tones and semitones, sharps and flats, major and minor.

The last of those three areas must, I think, be quite difficult to grasp if you don't play an instrument. In a sense they form the secret language of music. But they are not impossible to understand, and I hope this book will have helped to steer you through their complexities.

If you understand the basics about pitch, rhythm and keys, and grasp how these elements are represented on paper, in notation, then you can look at a page of printed music and comprehend a great deal of what you see.

Now let's just tidy up those 'odds and ends'.

REPEAT MARKS

There are various sorts of repeat marks. A pair of double bars with dots, facing each other, means repeat the enclosed passage, once, and then continue.

You might find the second double bar without the first:

This means repeat from the beginning. In other words, you don't need the dotted double bar at the very beginning of a piece, although it is sometimes inserted if the repeated section is very short.

First and second time bars

The first time, play the bar marked 1 and, as the repeat mark indicates, go back and repeat. The second time through, however, you *omit the first time bar* and jump to the *second time bar*, from which point you continue onwards.

Da capo, dal segno

D.C. stands for *da capo*, and means repeat from the beginning.

D.C. al Fine means: repeat from the beginning but go only as far as 'Fine' (pronounced 'feené', meaning 'end').

D.S. stands for *dal segno*, and means go back to the 𝄋 sign.

No prizes for guessing what this means: go back to the sign, then play as far as 'Fine' and stop there.

Even more complicated instructions are sometimes found, especially in pop songs. *D.S. al Coda* means repeat from the 𝄋 sign to another sign (𝕆), then jump to the *coda* (ending), which may be indicated by a second appearance of the second sign. If you think this is beginning to be a bit confusing, most musicians will agree with you wholeheartedly. In fact, if you see a player peering at a score with a puzzled expression, then leaning over to consult a colleague, they're probably trying to figure out which bits they're supposed to play in what order.

Repeat previous bar

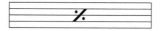

means repeat the previous bar.

EXPRESSION OR ARTICULATION MARKS

Staccato

A dot placed to the right of a notehead, as you know, multiplies its time-value by 1½. However, a dot placed *under* a notehead (or *over*, depending on which way the tail goes) means **staccato**: play the note in a short, detached way.

It's important to distinguish these two types of dots. In this example, the first, second and fourth bars contain dotted notes, but the third bar has notes which are to be played staccato:

Legato

The opposite of staccato is **legato**: play very smoothly. This group of five notes is marked to be played legato:

The curved line is called a **slur** or **phrase-mark**, and can be distinguished from a *tie* because it joins two or more notes of different pitches, whereas a tie always joins two notes of the same pitch.

Slurs are used in various specific ways, all of which are related to the general sense of *legato*. In a vocal part, a slur will show where a single syllable is spread over several notes, but you may also see longer phrase-marks which give the more general sense of the music's phrase-structure; long phrase-marks of that sort are also frequently found in piano music. For string instruments (violin, viola, cello, double bass), however, slurs have the specific purpose of joining notes which are to be played in a single bowstroke (i.e. without changing bow-direction). Likewise, for wind players a slur joins notes which aren't separately tongued. In both cases the effect is a smooth transition from one note to the next.

Other symbols or text instructions

Two common signs are:

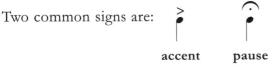

accent   pause

The **tenuto** sign   ![tenuto sign]   is also quite common. Technically it means 'sustain the note for its full value' (*tenuto* means 'held'), but in effect it is a kind of emphasis, asking the performer to lean on the note, or dwell on it slightly.

There are other signs, but most are more limited in their application. Some are instrument-specific, such as pedal-markings for pianists (showing when to apply the sustain pedal), or bowings for string players (showing whether to use an up-bow or a down-bow).

There are a also host of word-instructions a composer may use; for example, **dolce** (sweetly). Some imply tempo as well as the expressive character of the music; for example, **largamente** (broadly).

A composer doesn't have to use the standard Italian terms; but they have become an internationally recognised language, so have an advantage.

TEMPO (SPEED) MARKINGS

These generally appear at the head of a score, or at the beginning of a new section, if the tempo changes. For instance:

Allegro	fast
Andante	medium ('walking') pace
Adagio	slow

There are more, some being refinements that describe the *feel* required more precisely:

Andante sostenuto

Con spirito

The tempo might change during the course of the music:

rit. (*ritenuto*) or **rall.** (*rallentando*)	slow down
accel. (*accelerando*)	speed up

Many other terms are used for tempo or expression. A cheap, compact dictionary of musical terms is useful for quick reference.

DYNAMIC MARKS

These concern how loudly or softly the music is to be played. Among the most common are:

f	**forte**	loud
p	**piano**	soft
mp	**mezzopiano**	moderately soft
mf	**mezzoforte**	moderately loud
ff	**fortissimo**	very loud
pp	**pianissimo**	very soft
sf	**sforzando**	suddenly loud
cresc.	**crescendo**	getting louder
◁──────────		getting louder
dim.	**diminuendo**	becoming softer
──────────▷		becoming softer
fp	**forte-piano**	starting loud but immediately reducing to soft

There are others, including some different versions of the indication for *sforzando*, but those are the ones you'll encounter most often. More extreme dynamics can be marked: *ppp* and *fff* are not uncommon.

Modifying terms

Various terms can be used to modify tempi, dynamics or expression, for instance:

più	more	**meno**	less
subito	suddenly	**poco a poco**	little by little

ORNAMENTS

Other signs you might see include the following **ornaments**:

Trill

A rapid alternation with another note, normally the note above:

Grace note

A decorative note, normally played very quickly, squeezed in so that the rhythmic flow is not disturbed. It is printed smaller than the main notes:

Glissando

A slide, or smooth run (e.g. on a harp or piano), from one note to the other, touching all the other notes on the way.

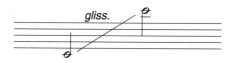

Spread chord

The notes of the chord aren't played quite together, but with a ripple-like effect starting normally with the lowest note. A common effect on piano or guitar.

TRIPLETS

Another sign – not an ornament – you may come across is a **triplet**: three notes played in the time of two. The example below shows a group of triplet quavers near the beginning of 'Amazing grace'. Other non-standard note groupings are also possible.

A - ma - zing——— grace

MORE ON TIME SIGNATURES

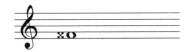

means the same as:

(This is because 4/4 time is also known as **common time**.)

Similarly:

means the same as:

DOUBLE SHARPS, DOUBLE FLATS

You won't often encounter them, but they do crop up occasionally. This is F double sharp:

And this is B double flat:

As you would surmise, F double sharp is a semitone higher than F♯, and that makes it the same as G. Likewise B double flat is the same as A.

Then why would we need them? Answer: in the same way as there is occasionally a need for E♯, the tonal context of a melody sometimes dictates that F double sharp is a more logical description of a note than G would be. Consider the famous introduction to the 'Shepherds' Farewell' by Berlioz:

In the double grace note leading into the first chord, the lower note is F double sharp leading to G♯. It wouldn't be sensible to write a G♮ at that point, like this:

POINTS TO REMEMBER

1 **Da capo** means go back to the beginning. **Dal segno** means go back to the sign.

2 **Staccato** means play in a short, detached way. **Legato** is the opposite: play smoothly.

3 A **triplet** is three notes played in the time of two.

4 **Common time** is another name for 4/4 time.

12

Case Studies

In this final chapter we will look at some examples of printed music and see how much we understand straight away – and also what problems or questions are thrown up.

PIANO MUSIC

Look at the example on the next page. How much can you tell yourself about it? Do you know what it is? Let's start interpreting this score.

Gleaning some basic information

Well, provided the information is trustworthy we know who wrote it, which is a good start. That position – just above the top line of music on the first page, on the right-hand side – is typically where the composer is credited, if at all. In fact it wasn't strictly necessary in this case, since the extract comes from a collection of Beethoven piano sonatas.

What about the other scraps of information next to his name? *Op.*, as you probably know, stands for *opus* (work), and in practice serves as a way of numbering a composer's publications. Beethoven's opus 27 was a set of two piano sonatas: hence Op.27 No.2.

We knew that this is piano music, but even if we didn't, the pair of staves, treble and bass, bracketed together, acts as a strong clue, even though there are other instruments (e.g. harp) which also appear that way.

Key, metre, tempo

The key signature has four sharps. Therefore the key must be either E major (see page 66) or C♯ minor (see the second paragraph on page 70). In fact the first bar consists entirely of notes from the C♯ minor chord (C♯, E and G♯), which again is a very strong clue, especially with the C♯ in the bass. Incidentally, while we're looking at sharps and flats, notice the D♯ in bar 4: it's a cautionary accidental (see page 75), marked because of the D♮ in the previous bar.

Now look at the time signature. The C with a line through it is a shorthand for 2/2 time (see page 99), so each bar has two beats and each beat is a minim. Notice that the key signature appears on every stave, but the time signature only at the beginning.

L. van Beethoven, Op.27 No.2

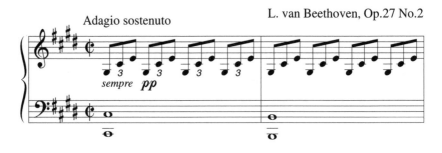

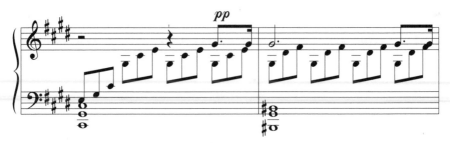

The pianist also has some instructions on how to play: *adagio sostenuto* (slow and sustained) and *sempre **pp*** (always very soft).

Troublesome triplets

Now we must look at the actual notes – and there are a few things that might seem puzzling. In the first place we see groups of not two but three quavers: but this is OK, because each group is marked with a 3, indicating that it is a *triplet*, i.e. three quavers played in the time of two (see page 99). In bar 2, however, the numeral 3s no longer appear, yet the quavers are still grouped in threes. Yes, the quavers are still triplets – otherwise there would be too many quavers in each bar – and the only reason there isn't a number three over each triplet is that the publisher considers it's obvious from the first bar: it's just a rhythmic pattern that continues unchanged. Strictly speaking the notation is 'wrong', but because of the context they get away with it; it's sufficiently clear.

Tune and accompaniment – all on one stave

Now look at bar 5. At the beginning of the bar the triplet pattern, because it's pitched so low, drops into the lower stave, though it would still be played by the right hand (the left is fully employed playing that semibreve chord underneath). Then the triplets move back to the upper stave, but with their stems downwards. Above the triplets there are some rests and (on the last crotchet of the bar) a dotted rhythm leading into the dotted minim in the next bar. This is the beginning of the 'big tune', even though it's all on one note at first. The right hand must manage to play both the triplet pattern, which is really an accompanying line, *and* the tune. Where two distinct lines appear on a single stave, as here, it is normal for the higher-pitched line to have upward note-stems and the other line downward note-stems.

Have you worked out what famous piece this is? (Answer on page 127.)

PIANO AND VIOLIN

The piece of music below is also Beethoven: the beginning of the 'Spring' Sonata in F. Notice that although there are two instruments instead of one, the music is constructed in a very similar way to the previous piece: melody at the top, slow-moving bass-line at the

bottom, and an accompanying line in the middle consisting of *arpeggios* or broken chords. In fact, rather like the previous piece, for the first two bars the piano part is built totally from the notes of an F major chord.

Instrumental parts

Why is the violin stave printed smaller than the piano? For one simple reason: we are looking at the pianist's 'part', i.e. the copy he or she plays from. The violinist's part, strangely enough, omits the piano altogether, and that's normal practice in chamber music.

The tiny numbers just above the clef on the violin stave are bar numbers, and they help the two players to rehearse together: 'Let's go from bar 58.'

Other points of detail

Notice the way the barlines go right across the two piano staves but break between the piano and violin. It's not terribly significant, and of course the piano and violin barlines are always vertically aligned, but it does help to separate the two instruments visually.

The repeat barline, with its dots, has its corresponding backward-facing repeat barline much further on, at the end of bar 86.

In bar 7, once again we have a cautionary accidental, the natural sign in front of the high D. Strictly speaking, the D$\sharp$ two notes earlier applies only at that pitch, not the upper octave. But the cautionary natural sign provides certainty; a performer might feel a bit unsure without it.

Look again at the score. We speak of this page as having three **systems**. Each system has three staves (two for the piano, one for the violin). To speak of 'lines' of music in this case would be ambiguous, and potentially confusing.

SONGS

The next four pages show some examples of how songs can be notated. The first example is not very much different from the violin sonata, in that there are two staves for the piano and one for the singer – though the singer's stave is full-size this time, as he/she doesn't sing from a separate part, but maybe from another copy of the same song book, or from memory.

The first two bars are an introduction, played partly to give the singer or singers their starting note and remind them of the tune. Once they have started, the piano part is a simple march accompaniment, once again based entirely on the notes of the key chord.

We see the beginning of the first verse. Sometimes the words of two or more verses are printed under the music, if the **underlay** (the match of syllables and notes) is consistent. For a song with many verses, verse 2 onwards will probably be printed below and separate from the music, laid out like poetry.

Two-stave versions

The version below shows the same melody incorporated into the piano part, and with the words also included, so that the whole thing uses only two staves. A pianist can play it, with the melody in the right hand, or a singer can sing from the same score. Chord symbols are included too, with guitarists mainly in mind – see pages 89–90.

A folksong for voice and guitar

Below you can see the beginning of *The Oak and the Ash*. Chord symbols and chord-shape diagrams are included, but no piano part. Notice the way the notes are *slurred* (see page 95) when there are two (or more) notes per syllable.

Pop and jazz notations

A classical song – say one by Schubert or Brahms – appears in an exact notated form, and always with a separate piano part if that's how the song was written. Pop songs, especially from the 1950s onwards, became known not from their sheet music but from records. As a result, their representation in print has inevitably been rather approximate.

The sheet music for pop songs usually includes an accompaniment for piano plus chord symbols – basically the same format as the score of 'John Brown's Body' on page 106, with the chord symbols added – but the intricate sound of a modern pop record often can't be replicated by a simple accompaniment of that sort; hence the difficulty of sitting at a piano and trying to get somewhere near the effect of the original record.

Alternatively the song may be printed as just melody plus chord symbols. Jazz standards, too, may appear in this way. If you pick up a jazz collection, don't be surprised if the chord symbols look a bit different from the ones you have encountered here; jazz players use a form of shorthand for their chord symbols, but you can quickly learn what the signs mean.

The collections available in music shops also include books that reproduce in near-exact notation instrumental solos that were originally improvised, whether in jazz, rock or blues style. These will be more difficult to read (and play) than a simple piano or chord-symbol accompaniment – but of course they are aimed at a more specialised market: saxophonists, electric guitarists, etc.

CHORAL MUSIC

Next, let's look at the first six bars of the 'Hallelujah Chorus' from *Messiah*.

There are a number of things to notice about this example. The line-up of voices is the usual one for a choir – sopranos, altos, tenors, basses – but what about the accompaniment? Handel wrote for choir and orchestra, not choir and piano.

Piano reductions

Answer: the score shown here is called a **vocal score**. It shows the vocal parts (both solo and choral) in their entirety, but turns the

orchestral parts into a **piano reduction**. This is very convenient for the singers, who don't need to see the instrumental parts in full detail, and also for use in rehearsal: the choir normally rehearses with a piano accompanist, and the orchestra only appears for the last one or two rehearsals.

Different scores for different purposes

A work like *Messiah* thus exists in several different printed forms:

◆ Vocal score, as described above.

◆ The conductor's score (or 'full score'). This shows all the parts – vocal and orchestral – in full detail.

◆ A 'miniature score' or 'study score'. This is simply a miniature version of the full score, more convenient for study. Sometimes people take miniature scores to concerts simply in order to follow the music while they are listening, though I think this is a rarer practice than it used to be.

◆ Instrumental parts. This is what the orchestral players have on their music stands. Each player sees only his or her music, and must count carefully in order to come in in the right place every time. Sometimes this entails counting umpteen bars of rests, while they have nothing to play – but orchestral players (especially the pros) have this down to a fine art.

Writing for tenors

There are a couple more things to mention before we leave the 'Hallelujah Chorus'.

Firstly, why is the tenors' music written in the treble clef? They're men, aren't they? Yes, but conventionally their music is written in the treble clef, but *sounding an octave lower*. If it were in the bass clef, an awful lot of it would use ledger lines: middle C and the notes just above. In fact every tenor note on page 111 would need at least one ledger line.

Vocal syllables

Secondly, why are all the choir's notes unbeamed, with separate quaver or semiquaver tails, when the notes in the piano accompaniment are beamed in the usual way? Answer: this is a matter of convention, and in fact the fashion is beginning to turn towards normal beaming throughout vocal parts. But it used to be that separate syllables were left unbeamed, while if two or more quavers were used for a single syllable they would be beamed in the same way as instrumental music.

The choral tradition

...is still very strong, especially in Britain but also in a number of other countries. If you like singing in choirs there is probably one nearby which will be pleased to have you. And many amateur choral singers are not terribly confident about their music-reading; they hope to stand/sit next to someone who knows the music well, and pick it up that way – and of course through the repetitive process of rehearsing.

If by any chance you're in that category, but you have worked through this book up to this point, I hope it will have helped to give you some anchorage points. Get out your score of *Messiah*, or whatever you're working on, and look at a passage. What key are you in? Look at when you are singing the keynote, when you are a third higher, or a fifth higher, and try to internalise what those notes sound like, relative to each other. Look at the rhythms, and how they fit against the basic beat.

HYMNS

Let's look at another type of choral music. Here are the first two lines of 'All people that on earth do dwell':

OLD HUNDREDTH   Genevan Psalter, 1551

Short scores

Instead of setting out the four parts (soprano, alto, tenor, bass) on four separate lines, as it was for the 'Hallelujah Chorus', this is yet another type of score, a **short score**, in which the four parts are condensed onto two staves. Stems up for soprano and tenor, stems down for alto and bass.

A short score, by its nature, looks rather like a piano score, though without the curved bracket. A pianist or organist can play straight from it; there's no separate accompaniment.

More tenor confusion

Guess what, the tenor line now appears in the bass clef! Yes, every rule has its exceptions, and short scores are exceptions for tenors. Rather luckily, in this case the tenor part lies quite low and doesn't need any ledger lines.

Texts and credits

The words of the hymn are not printed under the notes. Rather, they are normally printed further down the page, all the verses, in poetic form.

The name 'Old Hundredth' is the name of the tune. Nearly all hymn tunes have a name, and traditional hymn-books, at least, tend to print them in this manner. The composer (or source of the music, in this case), is credited at the top right (the usual place for a composer-credit) while the author or source of the words appears at the end of the text.

Line-splits

Expert music-readers among you may have noticed that some of the bars appear to have only two beats (a minim) instead of four, as the time signature would lead us to expect. Well, we're allowed to start with an incomplete bar (see *upbeats*, page 38), so that disposes of the beginning, but what about the end of the first line and the beginning of the second? The answer is that those two minims are really half-bars, despite the double barline. The words go like this:

> All people that on earth do dwell,
> Sing to the Lord with cheerful voice;

and those two lines match the two lines of music. If we strictly count off every four crotchets, 'dwell, Sing' belong in one bar, but in hymn-books it's normal to insert a double-barline at the end of each line of text, even if that comes notionally in the middle of a bar.

Still more tenor confusion

Strangely enough, just to confuse you even further, there is such a thing as a **tenor clef**, but only cellists ever have to read one of those, and sometimes bassoonists and tenor trombonists – and of course composers and conductors, who have to know everything. Well, yes, and arrangers, and copyists, and orchestral librarians...

Rest assured, even if you're a tenor you'll never have to sing from a tenor clef.

OPERA

The type of opera score you're most likely to see is a vocal score; therefore much that we've said about the 'Hallelujah Chorus' will apply in the same way. Let's look at an example – a dramatic moment from Mozart's *Don Giovanni* (see opposite).

Tremolo

The most puzzling thing here is the notes in the last two bars of the piano reduction, right hand. From the beams they look like semi-quavers, yet the note-heads are white, like minims. This is a special form of notation, and indicates *tremolo* (or *tremolando*), which is a rapid repetition or alternation of notes. It can be a shivering or shimmering effect, depending on the choice of notes and instrumentation.

Other points about this example simply reflect the practical intention of the score. Words are given in English and Italian. A typical opera vocal score also includes stage directions, even though there aren't any in this example. *Più stretto* means faster, and the double barline draws attention to the change of pace. 'G' and 'C' at the left-hand ends of the vocal staves stand respectively for 'Don Giovanni' and 'Commendatore', the two characters singing those lines.

ORCHESTRAL MUSIC

As mentioned, a conductor normally uses a full-size copy, while 'miniature scores' are convenient for study, or for following while listening.

On the opposite page you can see the first four bars of Beethoven's *Coriolan* overture. The instrument names run down the left-hand side; you may see these in various languages, and in abbreviated forms. The order is always the same: woodwind at the top, starting with the highest-pitched, then brass, then percussion, then strings.

Transposing instruments

One strange thing, though, is the assortment of key signatures. Surely the instruments aren't all playing in different keys? Not really: the *Coriolan* overture is firmly in C minor, which is why the predominant key signature here is three flats. But certain instruments – including clarinets, trumpets, horns and saxophones – are **transposing instruments**: that is, they read their part in one key but actually sound in a different key. A clarinet in B♭, for instance, sounds a tone lower than its part is written: if it reads C it plays B♭. The reasons for this apparently convoluted practice are basically historic. The timpani (or kettledrums) are *not* transposing instruments, but since they only play C and G in this piece, there's no need for their three-flat key signature.

Alto clef

And have you spotted the relatively unusual clef used by the viola? In this book you have encountered the treble and bass clefs; this is the **alto clef**, which is virtually only used for viola music.

POINTS TO REMEMBER

1 Scores vary not only from one type of music to another, but also according to the type of score, which in turn depends on who will be using it, for what practical purpose.

2 Songs may be notated on three staves, two staves or one stave, depending on whether there is a separate piano accompaniment, or one which includes the tune in the right hand, or melody and chord-symbols only.

3 **Piano reductions** are piano versions of what is otherwise played by an orchestra.

4 **Vocal scores** show voices (in full) plus a piano reduction.

5 A **short score** shows a four-part choir (soprano, alto, tenor, bass) on two staves (a bit like a piano reduction).

6 Tenor voice parts are normally written in the treble clef, an octave higher (except in short score, when they appear in the bass clef, with note-stems up).

7 Clarinets, trumpets, horns and saxophones are **transposing instruments**. They read their parts in different keys, and they sound lower or higher (depending on the transposition) than printed.

8 Violas use the **alto clef**.

9 A line of music in a score, especially if it contains more than one stave, is called a **system**.

A Final Word

You have come a long way. Whether you play an instrument, or sing, or are primarily a listener, your knowledge of music notation will be a pleasure to you, and a useful tool. As well as its practical applications for any performer, it will help to give you insights into how the music is put together, and you will have the feeling of knowing the music from the inside.

Glossary

Accidentals   Sharps or flats or naturals applied to an individual note, as opposed to when they are in the key signature.

Arpeggio   The notes of a chord played in succession instead of simultaneously.

Bar   Most music is divided up into *bars*, usually so that the predominant regular accent falls at the beginning of each bar.

Barline   A vertical line drawn across the stave, separating two bars.

Beat   The steady ticking pulse which, whether audible or not, underlies most (though not all) music.

Chord   Several notes played at once.

Chromatic   A chromatic scale consists entirely of semitones, i.e. using all the notes. More generally, 'chromatic music' includes lots of notes which lie outside the main key of the piece.

Clef   Appearing on the stave at the beginning of each line, it has the effect (and purpose) of fixing the pitch of each line and space.

Common time   4/4 (four-four) time.

Crotchet   A note-length (or 'note-value'), widely regarded as a basic time-unit in music, and often (though not always) the same as a **beat**.

Da capo   Repeat from the beginning.

Dal segno   Repeat from the sign.

Dynamics   Indications of loudness/softness.

Flat   The note a semitone lower; for instance B flat is a semitone lower than B. Can also mean lower-pitched in a general sense.

Harmony The vertical aspect of music: sounds in combination – as opposed to *melody*, sounds in succession, the horizontal aspect.

Interval The distance from one note (pitch) to another.

Key A piece of music is said to be 'in the key of...', relating to the scale which in some sense forms its basis: see Chapter 7 if that seems cryptic!

Keynote The home-note or basis-note of a scale or tune; the bottom note of the scale.

Key signature The sharps or flats written at the start of each stave.

Ledger lines Small horizontal lines used to extend the stave upwards or downwards.

Legato Smoothly.

Major A characteristic scale or chord, including a particular pattern of tones and semitones between its various notes.

Measure American terminology for **bar**.

Metronome A clock-like machine that ticks at any required speed.

Metronome mark A way of indicating the desired speed of the music.

Miniature score A full score, but printed small for study purposes.

Minim A note-length (or 'note-value'), equal to two crotchets.

Minor A characteristic scale or chord, including a particular pattern of tones and semitones between its various notes – distinguishable, for instance, from the pattern that characterises a **major** scale or chord.

Modulation Moving from one key to another.

Natural A sign cancelling a previous sharp or flat indication.

Note-value The relative duration of a note (crotchet, minim, etc.).

Octave The distance from one note to the next note (up or down) with the same note-name.

Opus number A way of numbering a composer's publications.

Piano reduction A version of an orchestral part to be played on piano.

Pitch How high or low a note is.

Quaver A note-length (or 'note-value'), equal to half a crotchet.

Relative keys (major or minor) Each major key has a relative minor, and vice versa.

Rests Silent spaces in the music. Rests are given time-values equivalent to notes (crotchet, quaver, etc.).

Rhythm A word with wide and general use in music, but specially referring to recognisable patterns of longer and shorter notes.

Scale A sequence of notes, rising or falling, usually spanning an octave.

Semibreve A note-length (or 'note-value'), equal to four crotchets.

Semiquaver A note-length (or 'note-value'), equal to half a quaver.

Semitone The distance between adjacent notes, e.g. E and F, or F and F♯ (F sharp).

Sharp The note a semitone higher; for instance F♯ is a semitone higher than F. Can also mean higher-pitched in a general sense.

Short score Sometimes the same as **vocal score**; also a score in which four vocal parts are set out on two staves (treble and bass).

Slur A curved line joining two or more notes which are to be played smoothly, or (for a wind instrument) not separately tongued, or (for a string instrument) not separately bowed.

Staccato Play the notes short, detached.

Staff Same as **stave**. Originally 'staff' was the singular, 'staves' the plural, but now the latter word is commonly used in a singular form as well.

Stave The five horizontal lines on which music is written.

Tempo Speed.

Tie A curved line joining two notes which are to be played as one.

Time signature An indication of the number of beats per bar, and the time-value of each beat.

Tone Two **semitones**.

Transpose To transpose a piece of music is to play it in a different key, but without otherwise changing anything. (Whereas to **modulate** is to move from one key to another *within* a piece of music.)

Transposing instruments These read their music in one key but actually sound in a different key.

Triplet Three notes played in the time of two.

Upbeat The last beat of a bar, which has the feeling of leading into the (strong) first beat of the next bar. The word is often used in situations where a melodic phrase *begins* on an upbeat.

Vocal score A score with vocal parts in full, plus piano reduction of the orchestral parts.

Whole-note The American term for a semibreve.

Answers to Questions

Pages 13–14

A D C F F A G D
E G F E C F A D
E B D C F F B A
E G G D A C B C
C E C B F A D G
A E B C F D B C
A C G E F D C G
D G B A D B C E
E D C F G B F D
B D A B F E C F

Middle C is printed four times: at the end of line 4, the beginning of line 5 (both on page 13), then the penultimate note of line 8 (the second line on page 14), and also the penultimate note of line 10 (the last line).

Pages 22–23

The fourth line (the second on page 23) has one quaver too many.

Page 39

All Through the Night

Page 40

Country Gardens; William Tell Overture

Page 52

Semitone
Semitone, tone, tone, semitone
Semitone, semitone, tone, tone

Page 53
C sharp, G sharp, D flat
F sharp, B flat, D sharp
Semitone, tone, semitone, semitone
Tone, tone, semitone, tone

Page 65
The notes of the E major scale are E, F♯, G♯, A, B, C♯, D♯, (E).
Therefore there are four sharps.

Page 67
Nos. 1, 4 and 5 are correct, representing the keys of A major, A♭ major and B major.
Nos. 2, 3 and 6 are incorrectly set out.

Page 70–71
The National Anthem; *Charlie is my Darling*

Page 103 (score on page 102)
The 'Moonlight' Sonata

Further Reading

The book trade and the music trade are two different things. Music shops sell instruments and sheet music, but also have a few books (ones that have been published by music publishers rather than book publishers). Good music shops are hard to find, but mail order and the internet have moved to fill the gap.

Books

The AB Guide to Music Theory Part 1, Eric Taylor, ABRSM Publishing (the publishing arm of the Associated Board, who run the best-known of the graded examination systems)

All Music Guide to Popular Music, Backbeat Books

British and International Music Yearbook, Rhinegold Publications

A History of Western Music, Donald Jay Grout and Claude V Palisca, Norton

Music Dictionary, Roy Bennett, Cambridge University Press

Music Explorer video with book, Richard McNicol, London Symphony Orchestra (available direct from the LSO's Discovery department)

New Harvard Dictionary of Music, edited by Don Michael Randel, Belknap/Harvard

Pop Music: the Text Book, Julia Winterson, Peter Nickol and Toby Bricheno, Peters Edition

The Rough Guide to Opera, Matthew Boyden, Rough Guides

Rudiments of Music, Stewart Macpherson, Stainer & Bell

The Student's Dictionary of Musical Terms, Arthur J Greenish, Stainer & Bell

What to Listen for in Jazz, Barry Kernfeld, Yale University Press

World Music: the Rough Guide, Rough Guides

Periodicals

BBC Music, Origin Publishing, www.bbcmusicmagazine.com
Classical Music, Rhinegold Publications, www.rhinegold.co.uk
The Gramophone, Haymarket Consumer, www.gramophone.co.uk
Music Teacher, Rhinegold Publications, www.rhinegold.co.uk

Books for children

I Wonder Why Flutes Have Holes (and other questions about music),
   Josephine Paker, Kingfisher
Instruments in Music (series), Heinemann
Usborne Introduction to Music, Eileen O'Brien, Usborne

Websites

www.bbc.co.uk/radio3/
www.bemuso.com/find/sitemap.html
www.musicweb-international.com/
www.sun.rbbnc.ac.uk/Music/Links/index.html
www.essentialsofmusic.com/
http://web.ukonline.co.uk/martin.nail/folkmus.htm
http://bubl.ac.uk/link/c/classicalmusiclinks.htm

Useful Addresses

Arts Council of England
14 Great Peter Street, London SW1P 3NQ. Tel: 020 7333 0100

Associated Board of the Royal Schools of Music
24 Portland Place, London W1B 1LU. Tel: 020 7636 5400

British Academy of Composers and Songwriters
British Music House, 26 Berners Street, London W1T 3LR.
Tel: 020 7636 2929

British Music Information Centre
10 Stratford Place, London W1C 1BA. Tel: 020 7499 8567

English Folk Dance and Song Society
Cecil Sharp House, 2 Regents Park Road, London NW1 7AY.
Tel: 020 7485 2206

European Piano Teachers' Association UK (EPTA UK),
Archpool House, High Street, Handcross, RH17 6BJ.
Tel: 01444 400852

European String Teachers' Association (ESTA)
105 Perryfield Way, Richmond TW10 7SN. Tel: 020 8940 4640

Incorporated Society of Musicians
10 Stratford Place, London W1C 1AA. Tel: 020 7629 4413

Making Music (formerly National Federation of Music
Societies), 2–4 Great Eastern Street, London EC2A 3NW.
Tel: 0870 872 3300

Mechanical-Copyright Protection Society
Elgar House, 41 Streatham High Road, London SW16 1ER.
Tel: 020 8664 4400

Music for Youth
102 Point Pleasant, London SW18 1PP. Tel: 020 8870 9624

Music Publishers Association
3rd floor, Strandgate, 18–20 York Buildings, London WC2N 6JU. Tel: 020 7839 7779

Musicians' Union
60–62 Clapham Road, London SW9 0JJ. Tel: 020 7582 5566

Performing Right Society
29–33 Berners Street, London W1T 3AB. Tel: 020 7580 5544

Pianoforte Tuners' Association
10 Reculver Road, Herne Bay, CT6 6LD. Tel: 01227 368808

Schools Music Association
71 Margaret Road, New Barnet, Herts EN4 9NT.
Tel: 020 8440 6919

Scottish Music Information Centre
1 Bowmont Gardens, Glasgow G12 9LR. Tel: 0141 334 6393

Sing for Pleasure
Bolton Music Centre, New York, Bolton BL3 4NG.
Tel: 0800 0184 164

Society of Recorder Players
6 Upton Court, 56 East Dulwich Grove, London SE22 8PS.
Tel: 020 8693 4319

Society of Teachers of the Alexander Technique
1st floor, Linton House, 39–51 Highgate Road
London NW5 1RS. Tel: 020 7284 3338

Sonic Arts Network
The Jerwood Space, 171 Union Street, London SE1 0LN.
Tel: 020 7928 7337

Sound Sense
7 Tavern Street, Stowmarket IP14 1PJ. Tel: 01449 673990

Voices Foundation
38 Ebury Street, London SW1W 0LU. Tel: 020 7730 6677

Youth Music
1 America Street, London SE1 0NE. Tel: 020 7902 1060

Index